BÔ YIN RÂ
(JOSEPH ANTON SCHNEIDERFRANKEN)

VOLUME 23
OF THE 32-VOLUME CYCLE
THE GATED GARDEN

ON
MARRIAGE

For information
about the books of Bô Yin Râ and
titles available in English translation,
visit the Kober Press web site at
http://www.kober.com.

THE KOBER PRESS PUBLISHES THE ONLY ENGLISH TRANSLATIONS
OF THE BOOKS OF BÔ YIN RÂ AUTHORIZED BY THE KOBER VERLAG,
SWITZERLAND. THE KOBER VERLAG PUBLISHES THE BOOKS OF
BÔ YIN RÂ IN THE ORIGINAL GERMAN AND HAS PROTECTED
THEIR INTEGRITY SINCE THE AUTHOR'S LIFETIME.

BÔ YIN RÂ
(JOSEPH ANTON SCHNEIDERFRANKEN)

ON
MARRIAGE

TRANSLATED FROM THE GERMAN
BY JAN SCHYMURA, MALKA WEITMAN
AND ERIC STRAUSS

BERKELEY, CALIFORNIA

This book is a translation from the German of *Die Ehe* by
Bô Yin Râ (J.A. Schneiderfranken) published in 1925 by
Richard Hummel, Leipzig. The copyright to the German
text is held by Kober Verlag AG, Bern, Switzerland.

Printed in the United States of America

International Standard Book Number: 978-0-915034-29-1

Typography and composition by Dickie Magidoff

Book cover after a design by Bô Yin Râ

CONTENTS

CHAPTER ONE

THE SANCTITY OF MARRIAGE

HOLY, THREE TIMES HOLY IS THE UNION of Woman and Man joined together and living in harmonious closeness in this earthly life.

Holy is the ardor of the sexes to unite in love!

Holy the mystery of procreation and of giving birth!

Holy is the invisible bond uniting that which has already come into being, so that it may make ready the place into which a new being can be born.

Blessed the man and woman capable of grasping such a mystery and of recognizing one another in loving union, just as the Source of all Being recognizes itself as Male and Female, eternally unified within the bond of love.

Blessed with happiness the home within which a true marriage has taken place, sealed before Eternity by human beings conscious of their dignity, which then becomes the Godhead's sublime temple here on earth.

A miracle filled with mystery has found fulfillment here, revealed only to a few on earth and veiled even from the very ones who brought it into being.

IT SOUNDS to me like greatest folly, far removed from any wisdom, when people speak of "spiritual perfection" wherever male and female avoid each other on their life-paths for the sake of some supposed higher spiritual development of their souls.

An incomplete being is seeking its completion without the slightest inkling that such fulfillment can only be attained through melding with its other part—physically separated from it here on earth but once united with it in the realm of Spirit.

Lamentable are all those men and women on this earth who are unable to find the compatible polar opposite with whom they would become whole once more, enhanced by gaining that which their own individual pole's vibration alone can never give them.

Lamentable, like much else on this earth, are those who feel themselves hindered from attaining a level of true spiritual development, the possibility of which lies latent in us all.

To THOSE who are true seers, it often seems that, in such cases, nature herself takes pity on those relegated to incomplete and unredeemed humanity by stimulating their imagination to create an idealized vision of the opposite sex that is in fact a fantasy. This fantasy becomes for them a pathetic substitute for the missing polar opposite needed as a balance for their single pole.

Whoever is familiar with the many tales of ecstatic and mystical experiences throughout history will have no difficulty recalling a multitude of examples.

To be sure, such experiences are interpreted as being most sublime and spiritual. However, these experiences should rightly be understood as the result of emotion originating in the physical body from the excitation of its nerves.

❦

No human beings here on earth, be they male or female, who are physically fit for marriage and not precluded due to an implacably hard fate or other serious, irremediable reason, will be able to experience their spiritual nature in its utmost clarity while in this earthly realm, so long as they willfully avoid the balancing of poles inherent in nature, where male and female complement each other.

No bargaining is possible here, and nothing can be twisted or interpreted to one's favor.

None of those on earth who suppose that they may achieve spiritual perfection and yet view marriage as a hindrance to progressing on the path, or even as something to avoid, can reach their goal. They may be blinded by their own unacknowledged self-indulgence or deluded by a false religiosity and so are mislead into believing that here, where divinity draws near in the most profound of ways, they must guard themselves against the devil's snares. Thus they attain an imagined state of "holiness" which is in truth a delusion of ascetic thinking and which has, unfortunately, brought harm to all who revere it, even in our day.

❧

To THE LIBERTINE, the holiest of human mysteries is merely an occasion for arousal and the stimulation of nerves in pursuit of pleasure.

Such individuals have lost their way. They do not feel the dignity of their humanity and recklessly defile what is most holy.

No less lost are those who wish to progress on the path to perfection yet fail to recognize that they have need of their polar opposite if they are to become whole.

Lost are all those foolish and arrogant individuals who actually believe their single state to be a guarantee that they are on the right path, and who even consider themselves superior because they foreswear the union of marriage, believing that abstention draws them closer to "the kingdom of heaven."

❧

To BE SURE, persons who are unmarried can also travel the path to perfection by themselves and thus may even reach their goal one day, but during their life on earth they never will find the fulfillment that marriage alone can bring.

They will remain incomplete and will only be able to achieve a partial perfection during their time on earth, no matter how they struggle. They will never reach the clarity of consciousness that can only be attained when human beings become whole anew through the union of male and female in a true marriage.

Unmarried individuals will only be able to achieve this partial perfection if they can bear witness before God that their choice to remain single was based on legitimate grounds, and was not merely the result of deluded thinking.

Few are the grounds that can stand before the judgment of God—far fewer than such deluded thinking would have us believe.

No one should base the decision to remain single on such grounds until they have sought counsel within themselves and contemplated deeply, and are certain that they have heard God's voice in the quiet of silent meditation.

On the other hand, no one should seek union with the opposite sex purely out of lust, and not until one has understood that such a union will only be a blessing when one is willing to bear responsibility for it in the realm of Eternity—regardless of whether one's partner is aware of and willing to assume such responsibility as well.

THE ABSURD idea that "marrying is good but not marrying is better" has been with us a very long time. The one who first uttered these words did indeed have deep insight into many hidden spiritual truths but, now, because of his spiritual authority, all who came after him are oppressed by the heavy burden it has laid on their conscience.

It is time that these deluded words, from an otherwise enlightened teacher, lose their power at last.

Even though marriage is considered to be a sacrament—that is, a means by which to realize one's inherent sanctity—celibacy is declared to be more "saintly" still. It is time to free marriage of this slander at last. It is time to reject the belief that a woman who remains a stranger to the highest and holiest fulfillment of her womanhood, is to be valued above one who chooses the honor of motherhood. And time as well to reject the false thinking that places the unfruitful man, consuming his masculine force in self-centered pursuits and thus robbing the earth of the worth of his blood, above the one who fathers new life here on earth.

It truly is time to protect marriage at its most sacred core, from those who hold the act of procreation to be impure—from those who have dared to usurp the ancient, pagan myth and depict humanity's most worthy, God-imbued individual as having been born of a virgin. They have not understood that ancient myths speak in veiled language of the divine birth that takes place in the heart—the birth of the Living God in the soul that has been impregnated by God—and *this* is the "the Son of God" that is begotten of the Holy Spirit.

Worthy of highest respect, therefore, is the woman who became the mother of a son whose light-filled teachings have the power to bring salvation to the whole world—if only people would act in accordance with them, to the extent that those teachings are still truly known.

The father of such a son deserves no less respect, for whoever sees the son sees also the one who fathered him. This, because inheritance of the blood is passed on to the child from the parents, who can only bestow what they themselves already possess.

To deny the role of the father's bloodline in procreation is yet another expression of the disrespect that proclaims celibacy to be more saintly than marriage.

To BE SURE, there is no true marriage when people live side by side without genuine caring, enslaved to their instincts and simply using one another to quench their sexual desires.

Neither is there a true marriage when a couple enjoys sexual intimacy but perceives a child as a threat to their lust.

A true marriage also does not exist when new life is conceived irresponsibly, without the prerequisite conditions that will nurture and bless its development.

Truly, there is on earth no other state of being that requires more self-mastery, more empathy for the other, and more sense of responsibility than a true marriage!

Only those who fulfill all the noble requirements that are asked of them here may hope to experience the joy of marriage, sought by so many yet found by so few. Most people believe that it is their "right" to be happy in marriage; they do not realize that marital happiness, just as all other happiness, must be *created*.

The rest of this book will be concerned with the true meaning of marriage and what it demands.

I will show that even though the effort to create a marriage as it ought to be requires a steadfast readiness, a disciplined will, and the cultivation of one's strength, it is, nevertheless, easier to create a good and happy marriage than all the unhappy marriages we see would lead us to believe.

May what follows serve as a preparation for those who are yet to be married.

Those who have already been married for a long time, whether they are happy together or if their happiness has dimmed, may select from my words whatever may still be helpful to them.

Those, however, who face the grave decision as to whether the marriage they once entered into joyfully and full of hope for happiness should now be dissolved, because every possibility for happiness appears to have died, should ask themselves, after reading this book, whether they feel entitled to take this step and whether they are willing to bear the responsibility for it before the judgment of Eternity.

Of course, a marriage that has been irreparably broken should not stand in the way of new happiness.

One should also not persist to the bitter end in a relationship that heaps one disappointment upon another and creates nothing but grief and heartbreak daily.

Still, many marriages have been dissolved that were not damaged to the degree that would justify taking this drastic step before God.

In many of these cases an earnest attempt at a fresh start could have laid the foundation for new and lasting happiness—if the bridges to one another had not been prematurely broken because one spouse was already contemplating the possibility for happiness with a new person.

May those who are willing to listen and who sense that these words concern them—pay heed!

But those who must remain unmarried, because it is their fate or because they cannot shoulder the responsibility for a marriage and therefore feel it their duty to remain single— let them lay this book aside, for it has not been written for them.

I am writing here for those who are not held back by an unalterable or god-given reason from seeking completion in the union of marriage.

My words are meant only for them.

I AM ALSO all too familiar with the foolish idea held by some misguided people that the sanctuary of marriage must be cast aside in order to find true freedom, like some ancient walls, greyed with age, that must be torn down in order to liberate those trapped within them.

I cannot caution strongly enough against such a ruinous delusion.

From the time when humans roamed the earth in wild, untamed herds—a time in which, to speak in plain and vulgar terms, a woman had to submit to any man who forced himself upon her—a long road stretches out into the distance, and leads at last to the sacred temple in the world of the Spirit, in which one man unites in marriage with one woman.

In marriage, the human being's animal nature is made to serve the Spirit, even if reluctant to willingly obey.

Even today millions have not attained this level of development. Entire peoples still see women as existing only to satisfy men's lust, or to bear them children, or even as beasts of burden that one may buy and sell like cattle, so that the number of women a man "owns" bears testimony to his wealth, just as his herds grazing in the fields. Those who have reached a higher level have long recognized the truth that only marriage, uniting one woman and one man, is in harmony with the divine law of the Spirit.

Woe to all those who undermine their own marriage through untamed lust, and are unable to appreciate a person of the opposite sex without feeling desire.

It is not mere happenstance but, rather, the result of clear intention, when a marriage that has been carefully guarded, and kept pure from the taint of sexual involvement with others, remains immune to the destructive plague that a few moments of untamed lust may loose upon it, and from the curse it casts over the generations that follow.

Nature herself shows us clearly and unmistakably here what she herself demands of human beings in our time.

All those who dare to wantonly intrude upon a marriage uniting one woman with one man, and who disrespect the commitment and vows of that marriage—whoever they may be and whatever reasons move them—burden themselves with heavy guilt, commit an offense against all humanity, and create confusion in the cosmic order.

Beyond all this, they bear responsibility for the enormity of desecrating the temple that arises in the realm of radiant Spirit whenever a true marriage has been established.

Only the grace of God can pardon such transgressors from the burden of guilt they carry, and only if they freely seek atonement, led by their own conscience.

A guilt no less great weighs on those who seek to destroy an institution they believe to be "outmoded"—because they themselves are not able to imbue it with vitality.

All efforts to create a new and different model for the union of the sexes here on earth are in vain: because the benefits to humankind of marriage between one woman and one man are grounded in the innermost structure of the Godhead itself.

Those who wish to tear down what sublime insight has brought into being do not know the consequences of their actions.

They would destroy a sanctuary of the Spirit, built with painstaking care over thousands of years by the wisest human beings of their time.

Were it to lay in ruins, millennia would have to pass before it could be built anew, if this were even possible.

CHAPTER TWO

LOVE

THE SACRED BOND OF MARRIAGE, AS I WOULD have it be understood, perfects itself, above all, within the embrace of love, and cannot survive without love. Let me, therefore, dedicate the words I will speak here to love.

I shall speak first of a form of love that, although it manifests itself here on earth in the physical realm is, in truth, deeply rooted in the Spirit's realm.

This form of love can also be found in animals and in everything that lives.

Animals, however, are not able to sense the spiritual source of this love and so remain confined to its most instinctual level: the urge to mate that arises from the rhythm of the estrous cycle; the instinct for motherhood and concern for the litter.

Unfortunately, human beings are all too often enslaved—in precisely the same way—to the animal aspect of their own nature, with no desire to elevate themselves and learn to master the instincts and drives that rule them.

Those who can see the true nature of things are filled with pity when they behold such lamentable self-abasement—a level of existence content to satisfy itself with lust and brutish pleasures—while the power to experience the most sublime and holy joy lies within reach.

MANY INDIVIDUALS who feel some sense of their dignity, even if they cannot yet see the full depth of the divine in all Being, are repelled when they witness such desecration of the very word "human being."

This leads some to conclude that any love that arouses the energies of their animal nature must be of the same base level. They are unable to understand that their animal drive can be a gateway to spiritual heights.

And so they curse the fate that forces them to feel the pulse of the animal coursing through their veins, yet can never wrest themselves completely free of its power.

Thus tormented, they succumb to the delusion that all love that presses to express itself physically in them must be the spawn of Hell, and threatens to destroy their soul.

Where can they look for guidance that would shed light on these matters and put an end to their self-torment?

On one side of them are those who seek to bolster their delusion, because they themselves are enslaved to it as well; on the other side are those who ridicule them for it.

But those who have been granted the joy of experiencing the highest bliss—the joy of a love uniting animal with Godhead, which purifies the instincts so that they serve the longings of the soul—seldom ever speak of this most sacred experience.

Nowhere else is guidance more needed than on the path of earthly love, where poisonous plants grow wild, adorned in the same glowing colors as the purest, chalice-like flowers that hold the dew of heaven in their depths.

One need not look far to find individuals who can do no more than smile with bitter irony, whenever they hear love praised.

Marriages in which spouses have experienced such love are rare, although such love should be the norm for every marriage.

Some believe that love should realize its fulfillment within the soul alone. They are locked in battle with their body, and come to loath it, because they must suppress its cravings. And yet, deep down, they long for something different.

There are others who believe that love can only be enjoyed through satisfying their desire—until, satiated, they have no further need of their lover.

Neither of these approaches is the right way to experience the form of love a true marriage requires.

The only kind of love that is in harmony with the Spirit's law must embrace both love's physical and spiritual nature, and not forgo one for the other.

We should not enjoy our animal nature in a crude and brutish way but, rather, feel it to be permeated by Spirit, transformed and lifted to the realm of the Spirit's light.

In this way, man and woman, merged in body and spirit, are able to behold themselves within each other's being, just as Male and Female were once united in the godly realm, before the Fall into this world of matter—and to glimpse how Male and Female will be once again united when these two poles that together form the undivided human being are redeemed within the Spirit's realm.

Libertines will have no understanding for these words, nor, in the same way, will ascetics, who sense in every stirring of their animal nature only devilish temptation.

But those who have even only once experienced within themselves what my words seek to convey will surely understand their meaning.

And those who are pure of heart, but have not yet themselves experienced the sacred mystery that reveals itself through sexual union, will intuitively understand what can only be fully known once it has been felt.

❧

EACH MAN and woman will find fulfillment only in this highest spiritual-physical experience, in which together they become a unified, new being. Only this kind of union, encompassing far more than animal desire, can fully satisfy the intense longing of body and soul that draws the sexes to each other with love so strong that each forgets its own self and merges with the other.

Only in a true marriage, which enfolds Male and Female within a new unity and is entered into, with serious and firm intention, for the lifetime of both individuals, can a couple's sexual union reach these heights.

Even so, only through the utmost discipline of the senses and reining in of fantasies can this unfathomable mystery be realized.

❧

TO BE SURE, in every true marriage the desire for a child is a much wished-for goal.

And yet, according to the spiritual law that is to be fulfilled through marriage, begetting and giving birth to a new life is not the main purpose of marriage but, rather, only a secondary one.

The main purpose of marriage is the creation of a new entity within the Spirit, in which Male and Female are united and melded into one. This new entity can only be experienced, during life on earth, through the conjoining of physical and spiritual senses. Such union brings about an increase in life energy for both individuals, which neither could achieve alone, no matter how hard they might try.

Marriage is the only way to satisfy the deepest longings for the purest spiritual-physical love, and thus offers sublime help on the path to perfection. It is a mystery-filled preparation for the return to the realm of radiant, substantial Spirit, a gateway through which one may glimpse the bliss of transcendent life—if one is willing to use the key offered in this book.

If mortal humans were made of spiritual—not physical—matter, they would be able to experience all that marriage makes possible within their spiritual body alone.

Human beings, however, have fallen from the exalted heights where they once stood, god-like and filled with light. Turning away from the god that had been born in them at the Origin, they presumed that they themselves were gods, and so became imprisoned in their animal nature—forced to experience themselves in the realm of the physical senses. Thus, they now can only sense the spiritual through the physical energies that are a part of that animal nature.

And should they believe themselves freed of their animal nature—even though it is an animal body that carries them during their time here on earth—then they are merely deceiving themselves and impeding the development of their spiritual life. They falsely suppose they are having spiritual experiences when, in fact, the sensations they so value are merely arising within the animal self.

There is no better protection from such false interpretations than a true marriage, in which spiritual-physical love is realized in its purest and most sublime form.

❦

Y<small>ET THIS KIND</small> of love, which in a true marriage guides and governs every aspect of life together, is not expressed exclusively through the spiritual-physical bond, which is linked to the longing of the sexes for union.

While it is true that spiritual-physical love is always a prerequisite for a true marriage —for without it such a union is debased and the marital bond becomes a mere mockery of itself—the lives of those two married individuals who are fully aware of their unity in the Spirit are also illuminated by another form of love.

I am speaking of a form of love that needs no object in the outside world—a love that flows without an object.

This kind of love, too, can only be felt through the physical body and is made known to us through the bodily senses.

While the spiritual-physical love that leads to the union of the sexes always requires an other in order to discover itself in the glow of sexual passion, and even the love with which parents enfold their child and which is then reflected back onto them is not without an object—the kind of love of which I speak is completely free of attachment to an object and longs for nothing in the outside world. Nor does it require love in return, because it finds fulfillment in itself.

Not many know this kind of love!

It does not often manifest in life on earth.

And yet this kind of love is far more frequently encountered than the highest form of love in marriage.

This is because it can flow forth in any circumstance, and is not limited to marriage.

However, a marriage must not be without the kind of love that needs no object, if it is to be truly happy.

EVEN THE smallest, humblest hut is transformed into a temple when man and woman unite within it, sanctified by the highest form of spiritual-physical love. Yet, the life of two human beings joined in marriage does not take place only in the sacred temple of their home.

True marriage is an all-embracing sharing of life.

With every step they take, this life on earth will remind each partner that, despite the bond of body and spirit that they share, they remain two separate beings in the outer world —two separated parts of a single spiritual whole—and each is subject to the dictates of his or her own nature.

Two separate lives thus face each other, and are now to be melded into a new life of unity.

They must harmonize their lives so as to be united in the outer world just as they are within the spiritual-physical bond, if they would be happy in their daily life and not drive that happiness away.

Spiritual-physical love cannot help two individuals with the task of harmonizing daily life. And here we have laid bare the root of the misconception that there exists an innate "war" between the sexes.

❧

Do not believe this misguided notion, my friends! Such antagonism is not grounded in gender, even if it manifests at times when individuals of different genders live together.

In such cases, two different kinds of will are pitted one against the other. On the one side is the desire for erotic union, on the other is the self-centered wish to have one's own needs and wants rule the relationship.

Hatred may result from this conflict. But it would be wrong and unjust to interpret this hatred as natural or inherent in the relationship between the sexes.

Such hatred can only be vanquished by the love that needs no object—the self-fulfilling love whose flame is lit without an object.

Only this kind of love—love that exists for its own sake alone—will help both partners in a marriage find the right way to mold and polish one another, so that each is able to live in harmony with the other, blended together in a unified whole.

Even in many so-called marriages that merely borrow that name from true marriage, an acceptable level of harmony is often realized, if love for its own sake is felt by both spouses or even just by one—even if spiritual-physical love has not reached its highest expression or hardly exists in lesser forms.

❧

ONE OFTEN hears tales of "passionate love" that later "cools."

But true love never cools because its light-filled ardor is kindled by a source so rich that it can never be exhausted.

It may become a wild fire of passion but never can it be extinguished. Even if one tries to snuff it out with every means available—never can it cool!

There exist other ardent feelings, entirely different than this glowing love, that are nevertheless mistaken for love. Such passion may be stirred by an intoxication of the senses or an eroticism aroused by fantasy or artifice. It may lead one to mistake friendship for love, or misinterpret admiration or gratitude.

None of these have anything in common with true love excepting the word "love" itself.

No one should be surprised when such pseudo-love sooner or later cools.

Such artificially fostered feelings must never gain so much power over human beings that they are beguiled into believing that there is now a sound foundation for marriage.

❦

GREAT MISFORTUNE would be avoided if men and women whose paths have chanced to cross did not fixate on every erotic stirring between them, thus giving these feelings more power, and fooling themselves into thinking these feelings are "love."

Subtle waves of erotic energy flow at all times between every man and woman, and this is as nature would have it. These waves of energy are so faint that in more mature souls —those individuals whose focus lies far beyond mere physical existence—they are barely even noticed.

Danger is present only when unstable individuals, those who know not the discipline and restraint of pure hearts, focus on these subtle vibrations and give them power, letting their fantasies and senses run wild, until their excitement is felt as desire.

This desire is what they then call "love," and they believe this "love"—the product of an unrestrained imagination— to be the basis for a marriage. Feeling so entitled, they pursue the object of their erotic feelings with single-mindedness, completely lacking any sense of responsibility for their actions. And once they have attained their goal, their passion fades. They withdraw affection from the marriage partner once so ardently pursued, and are oftentimes already lured by a new object of desire.

I NEED HARDLY add that in such cases, it is most often men who desire a woman, for seldom is a woman's imagination so debauched that she will follow this same path.

Those who believe they know a woman's nature to be different than this may be reminded that such understanding doubtless comes from men who find it convenient to see their own nature reflected in the opposite sex. That is, unless these men have only known promiscuous women, and so suspect that every woman is promiscuous at heart.

Quite often a woman, too, may allow herself to be persuaded to enter into a marriage without love, and is later heard to bitterly lament that she has not found happiness.

More often, however, a woman brings about her own misfortune for other reasons, and these are frequently more forgivable than those that motivate a man.

The desire to capture the heart of a man she admires before another wins him, the wish to be taken care of or to flee an oppressive parental home—these are usually the reasons that propel a woman into a marriage without love. And if the play of erotic energy between her and her intended can be sufficiently intensified, then it can serve as a substitute for love.

THIS SORT OF marital "bond" can never be more than a caricature of a true marriage, and often does not last beyond a few years—no matter which side carries the heavier burden of responsibility for entering into a false marriage.

The spiritual law that demands absolutely to be complied with whenever Man and Woman wish to join in matrimony cannot be bent or broken in the way a marriage can be bent or broken. In truth, there never was a marriage if it can be undone this way, even if both partners once believed they were truly married and continued to believe so until the trials of life tested the foundation of their union.

❧

IF ONE WOULD have a true marriage, one must first be sure there is true love!

True love is easy to recognize and impossible to conceal.

It is never too soon to tear oneself away from nursing dreams of a pseudo-love. And one can never be too disciplined in avoiding any action that might encourage such delusion in another person.

❧

TRUE LOVE is not just a "feeling"; it is vast and exists beyond feelings alone.

Above all, love is energy, love is power.

Whoever misuses this power will come to know its other side: the energy of love will manifest as hate.

In such a case love appears as a distortion—a twisted image of itself.

But those who feel within themselves the power of love in its highest and most sublime form radiate this love, and surely will awaken it where it lies dormant in another, the moment they become aware they have encountered the person fate has chosen for them as their partner in true marriage.

When both partners deeply feel that a genuine love unites them, then the basis for a marriage truly exists.

Blessed with happiness is every marriage that is built upon such a foundation.

No storm that rages round such a marriage can ever shake it, nor can the strongest ocean breakers wash it away.

CHAPTER THREE

MARITAL HARMONY

LIVING TOGETHER IN CLOSEST PROXIMITY DOES not necessarily create closeness in a married couple, while close harmony often exists in cases where necessity dictates that the spouses remain apart for long periods of time, often against their wishes, and are only infrequently able to live under the same roof.

And while close harmony does not depend on sharing the same dwelling, every couple united within a true marriage will seek to live together whenever circumstances allow, taking into account the need to earn a living, and the responsibilities of one's profession and position in life.

It is one thing, however, to live together in the same home simply because one cannot bear to be alone, and quite another to live in closest harmony.

Harmonious closeness, as I speak of it here, is the union of two individuals encompassing all of their being, in feelings and actions and thought.

Living together does not of itself bring about this kind of closeness.

When harmony does not already exist in a relationship, in both inner life and everyday concerns, living together will not create that much-desired harmony, but may instead give rise to the thorniest of problems.

For this reason, it is essential that those who wish to join in matrimony strive first to cultivate close harmony before the marriage takes place.

Much harm has come to pass that could have been prevented had couples recognized in time that such a step cannot be bypassed, instead of indulging in the naïve belief that the harmony a true marriage requires will come about of itself, as a natural result of married life.

❧

THE STRIVING to create a harmony of feeling, thought and ways of dealing with the world can never be successful if either partner constantly engages in a tournament of words, a contest to convince the other of the correctness of their view, believing that their partner must concede the point in order for harmony to be restored between them.

One partner may, in this way, tire the other out and force the other to give in for the sake of peace. But this apparent harmony is no harmony at all and, sooner or later, there will be a price to pay.

Force can never foster harmony within a marriage, and giving in "for the sake of the relationship" does not contribute to the needed closeness. Marriage thrives on harmony as much as it does on love.

IF YOU, MY FRIEND, who are in love, wish to create the kind of harmony with your beloved in which all your thoughts and feelings blend and you agree about your dealings in the outside world, then you will have to, above all, practice firm self-discipline.

You must learn to become more flexible and to adapt yourself to some else's rhythm.

Up until this time you have been accountable to no one but yourself.

Whether you have adopted the values and beliefs of your parents and their ways of dealing with the world, or whether you have formed your own unique principles to guide you through life, you will always be inclined to over-value your perspective and to see everything you come across through the color of the lens of your own glasses.

But now my friend, a second person stands before you who, just as you do, sees the world through their own lens, colored differently than yours.

You must both resolve to take your "glasses" off, even if they allowed you each to see the world in the most beautiful of colors, so that now you can scarcely believe that anyone could see it otherwise.

❧

You must not expect that you can learn to understand each other from one day to the next; for even though you may both use the same words, you will always be speaking of different things, because each of you perceives the world in your own particular way and will thus describe it through the lens of your own vision.

You will hardly be able to believe that, truly, each of you perceives each thing in a completely different way.

You still believe that you are speaking of the same thing when you are actually speaking of something entirely different—since each person is describing only their own mental image of the thing.

Firm and steady patience is needed here, if both of you desire to one day see things in the same way.

Each of you must come to realize that our own way of perceiving—which up until now has seemed to be the norm—is by no means the only possible perspective.

You should not simply listen to the other's words but also always try to feel what the other person means by them and whether that meaning is what you suppose it to be—what you yourself would have meant had you chosen those same words.

❦

ONE ALL TOO often hears people arguing bitterly, convinced that they have irreconcilable differences, when in truth the wrong choice of words has created the impression of disagreement where it does not exist.

People often believe that a deep chasm separates them when in fact that "chasm" is a shallow ditch, arbitrarily dug and easily crossed. Only the night of ignorance obscures their vision and prevents them from seeing through this falsehood.

However, with imperturbable calm and loving tolerance they will find the way to each other at last, even where differences existed, even when a deep chasm seemed it would divide them forever, until they learned to build a bridge between them.

❦

HARMONY IN thought, feeling, and actions in the world creates a high protective wall around a marriage, surrounding it with safety.

Marriage cannot be sustained without a safe enclosure, tended to with care, that protects it from the outside world.

The union of two lives in marriage must never be exposed to the winds and storms of weather's fury.

No matter how much a married couple may enjoy their social life and the cheerful company of friends, they must always feel embraced within the safe enclosure of their marriage, and the sacred province that is theirs alone must remain intact and closed to any others.

Here too, as with every human relationship, the ability to remain silent is an art, and should be learned by anyone who has not yet mastered it.

MATTERS THAT concern only the married couple must not reach the ears of others, even if these others be their closest friends and relatives, or even their parents.

The "help" one might find in this way is likely to be questionable, even if the persons in whom one has confided have the best of intentions.

Far more often, however, seeking help from others has the opposite effect. By discussing their problems with others, the troubles the couple is trying to prevent instead proliferate and spread. Whereas, had they but made the effort to resolve private matters themselves, the rifts between them might have been swiftly mended.

IN THE SAME WAY, a married couple should keep their happiness to themselves, and not cause it to dissipate through mindless talk.

They should resist the temptation to speak of their happiness to others.

The happiness they created by becoming a unified whole in the Spirit is their concern alone.

Above all, they should guard against arousing the envy of others—which lies dormant beneath the surface and is all too easily awakened—by a loquacious tongue that extolls their marital happiness.

Envy harms the envious person as well the one who is envied, because it releases a destructive force that negates the treasures possessed by the envied one and which the envious person desires to possess.

❧

IF KEEPING SILENT with regard to one's happiness or troubles is important, then silence is even more essential in the face of shallow banter and obscene backstairs humor, or the tasteless teasing that feeds on deriding others, that would drag marriage into the gutter, bereft of spiritual substance.

Anyone who reads this will easily recognize exactly what I mean.

Let no one think that such crass, dull-witted jesting should be tolerated, even if it comes from someone who otherwise cannot be accused of impugning the sanctity of marriage.

That which is sacred must never be permitted to become the subject for vulgarity or jest. Even seemingly harmless humor may taint it, and so must be reined in so that it does not cause unintentional harm.

Only when human beings can sense the holiness of things are they still able to connect to life's sacred dimension. The sacred must always be protected from demeaning talk and sheltered from anyone or thing that cannot approach it with due reverence.

ॐ

THE HALLOWED province that belongs to the two spouses, and which no one else may enter, extends beyond their bedroom walls.

It encompasses many things that in and of themselves would not require concealment.

Closeness in a marriage dictates that many matters not directly related to the marriage also be concealed from the outside world.

Absolute trust is required to sustain this closeness. One must always be able to face the other partner just as one would face oneself.

Mockery or derision has no place in a harmonious marriage.

Loveless and sarcastic comments are never uttered where harmony abides.

Closeness in a marriage depends on the commitment of the partners to take care of one another; each must use their strengths to balance out the weakness of the other and so help each other through this life.

Harmonious closeness is possible only when both spouses know they need not hide from the other that which they acknowledge in themselves.

Only in this way can the practice of closeness in marriage become the school in which both spouses pursue the study of their own perfection in the inner world.

Love and forbearance will achieve but little unless there is absolute certainty that the portal to this school is firmly closed to outsiders and open only to the couple who seek to learn from one another within its walls.

Each partner must feel confident of this protection, and free of fear that one day, during an unguarded moment, their spouse may indulge in idle talk and inadvertently reveal their confidences to others.

There must never be a danger that other ears may hear of things the spouses have entrusted to each other.

Many tender shoots of closeness have been destroyed by such thoughtless talk, just as they were beginning to take root.

❧

A HARMONIOUS MARRIAGE must enfold within its closeness all the adversity and suffering that may befall either partner, even if the other is not affected or fails to understand its impact and the discouragement it causes.

In such cases, the unaffected partner may be unable to help carry the burden, but even here the *willingness* to help can still be present, and will offer comfort to the sufferer.

One should not shirk from such a willing readiness to help, even if one does not feel capable of helping—because the *willingness* to help is helpful in and of itself.

Closeness cannot be sustained as long as spouses feel resentment towards each other. If either spouse feels that he or she has been left to carry a burden up a mountain all alone, while the other remains impervious to this distress—the taste of bitterness will poison the relationship. It does not matter whether the burden is real or as heavy and oppressive as imagined—what matters is the willingness to help the partner who is suffering.

It goes without saying that couples should bear their troubles together whenever fate places a burden of suffering on both their shoulders. However, when suffering affects only one partner in a marriage, the deepest love is sometimes not enough to move the other to fulfill their duty to share their loved one's grief. Yet they must find the strength within them and rise to meet this duty, even if they cannot fully understand the other's suffering.

IF YOU SEEK happiness in marriage, then strive for closeness and harmony in all aspects of life that you can experience together, and extend the boundary of those things that you would share farther out than you might think possible.

It behooves each partner in a marriage to take an interest in matters that concern the other, even if they had no such interest at the start.

And it is equally important to give the other insights into unfamiliar matters, so that they might learn to understand them.

You should also be aware, however, that each soul has certain regions that cannot be laid open to even the closest other soul.

Duty also often demands that certain things remain concealed and, in such cases, you must trust your partner and respect the fact that these things cannot be shared with you.

Such trust will come easily to you if, in all areas of marriage where sharing is allowed, absolute trust already exists between you and the polar opposite with whom you are united.

Beware of curiosity that would entice you to force your way into areas of life you have no right to enter, and where duty demands that the key be withheld from you.

In a true marriage, however, one should still be able to sufficiently inform the other of the nature of those things one cannot share, so that there will not be a tear in the fabric of the couple's life of trusting closeness.

Where mutual trust prevails, suspicion will never be aroused, even when matters that cannot be expressed, or must not be communicated because of a duty to be silent, are spoken of in only the most general way. Nor will a truly loving partner insist on digging deeper into areas that are not theirs to know.

On the other hand, one should not intentionally allude to secrets one is keeping in order to titillate the other person's curiosity, or lend an air of mystery to oneself.

Only a complete fool would behave this way, and such conceit will surely lead to unintended consequences.

If true harmony is to be nourished and sustained, then those matters that one partner keeps concealed—yet would gladly speak of if they could—must be regarded with respect and even held in high esteem.

When this respect is present, each partner will be content with what the other shares with them and truly, it will suffice to secure the couple's closeness, even in their innermost life. For no soul on earth can ever express everything that it may experience, and this understanding is essential in a marriage.

CHAPTER FOUR

SORROW AND JOY

THERE HAS NEVER BEEN A MARRIAGE THAT has known only happiness and never was touched by sorrow.

Sorrow and joy are always mixed together in life on this earth, and may make for some a bitter brew. And although it is up to us to choose the attitude we take towards what life brings us, we can never avoid suffering and choose only joy.

Especially in marriage, the efforts we make to minimize suffering and increase joy are deeply meaningful.

The reality of suffering and the sorrows of life cannot be made to disappear, and no kind words of comfort can free us from the trials we must endure.

Those who try to do so think that suffering can be driven out by happiness, as if one could replace the other.

And yet, we do have the power to help restore happiness. We do have the power to increase joy on this earth.

THERE IS NO need to tell human beings how to bring more suffering into the world; even if no person had ever caused pain to another, there would still be suffering on this earth. This is because every living thing in the external world fights for its own existence, and can only maintain itself at the expense of others.

It is folly to presume that there is any way to banish suffering from this world, and those idealists and compassionate dreamers who think that they can do so are naïve. Suffering is inherent in the laws of nature, because every living thing displaces space and occupies it for itself alone.

Suffering is present in the very act of creation, when the outer world fragments the seamless unity of space and gives birth to form. The only way to banish suffering is to destroy all outer worlds—but if this were to ever come to pass, all inner worlds would also be destroyed.

❧

THIS OUTER-MOST of outer worlds—the world we can only perceive through the senses of this physical body in whose animal nature we are imprisoned—is filled with suffering.

And vast regions of the unseen realms of this outer world are in the same way exposed to suffering—indeed, sometimes even more so—because, here too, everything exists only by displacing space and occupying it for itself alone. But there also exist countless inner worlds in which there is no suffering, because here all being is open and interpenetrates, and the vast expanse of space remains unbroken in a seamless whole.

Those worlds that exist through separation and where suffering is therefore present, can never be freed from it. All human efforts to alleviate the suffering of this world through self-renunciation, suppression of human needs, or idealistic attempts to deny the realities of existence will fail, and will only serve to anesthetize one's feelings of compassion.

In life on earth, the power of human beings is limited: they can add needless pain to the world or diminish it. But this earthly realm can never be entirely released from suffering, if the outer world and, with it, every inner world are to exist.

❧

HUMAN BEINGS do have the power to free themselves of suffering and sorrow that they bring upon themselves. We can, indeed, avoid much suffering and sorrow if we use this power wisely.

We also have the power to spare our fellow human beings much needless suffering and pain.

In every human encounter, it is our duty to lessen our own pain and that of our fellows.

Even human beings who have never met before and who will never in this life meet again must recognize this obligation to each other. How much more binding and holy, then, is this same duty between two persons who have united in a marriage, in order to complement and perfect one another.

Here, where woman and man live together in close harmony, each aware of all the troubles that may cause the other pain and each knowing where the other is most liable to be injured, there exists the greatest opportunity to shield the other person.

_℘_

MARRIAGE CAN be a fountain of happiness but it can also become a clouded pond of sorrow.

Each partner must regard it as their highest goal to foster the happiness of the other. Those who do not do so may inadvertently forfeit their own happiness as well.

Those who truly love would rather suffer themselves than see their partner suffer.

No hardship will seem too difficult to them if they know that through their efforts they can alleviate their loved one's pain.

The alleviation of suffering alone, however, is not sufficient.

Humanity's highest and most noble duty is fulfilled only when one actively brings joy to another.

And where can one more perfectly fulfill this loving duty than in marriage?

❧

IN THE LIFE of every marriage there are abundant opportunities for creating happiness, if one will only seek them out and use them. Such joyful moments can banish sorrow and dispel the clouds of threatening storms.

Each partner in a marriage should try to feel what the other person longs for and what it is that gives them joy, and not assume it is the same as what they themselves desire. Even the best of intentions will miss the mark if you are guided solely by your own desires.

That which brings you greatest happiness may seem unimportant to your polar opposite, and your partner may feel deepest happiness where you remain unmoved by any feeling.

However often or how badly you may err in trying to please your partner, you must not allow yourself to feel hurt, even when your carefully and lovingly conceived surprise does not delight as you intended.

If you are to learn from this experience, then you must give the matter thought and realize that you have failed to empathize with the other person. For even if the closest harmony unites the two of you, you each abide within the realm of your own feelings, and the rhythm of those feelings will determine what at any given moment seems of value or a source of joy.

Therefore, do not look to your own self when your intention is to make the other person happy.

If you wish to be a source of joy, you should delight in making others happy in the ways that *they* desire.

IF YOU DOUBT your ability to be a source of joy, your attempts to bring happiness to others will be in vain.

You should never think that you will not now succeed because you did not succeed in the past.

YOU MUST FIRST become happy yourself, if you would bring happiness to your partner!

For only when one is filled up with happiness can it overflow to grace another.

Dive deeply, therefore, into yourself so that you may discover a wellspring of constant joy that lives within you. Your happiness will then no longer be dependent on events outside of you, although you should welcome such external gifts whenever they present themselves.

The kind of joy that you can best transmit to others is not caused by anything in the outside world.

This kind of joy will spread more happiness than any caused by things outside yourself.

Do not forget the little gestures that can bring each other joy, the opportunities that each day holds in store.

Regard nothing as too insignificant if you can use it to delight the other.

Small gestures often bring the greatest happiness.

In married life each day contains a thousand opportunities to make each other happy—

if only for a moment—by inventing small delights.

One should not let any opportunity pass by without making use of it!

In a truly happy marriage you will observe that each partner finds inspiration for creating little pleasures in each hour of the day.

A skillful gardener will never fail to notice even the small blossoms that border the most colorful and glorious flowerbed, no matter how modest they may appear.

And so it is with marriage. If you wish to make the most beautiful harmony in the flower garden of your marriage, the smallest opportunities for creating happiness should not be overlooked.

THE SUFFERING and sorrow that a married couple will have to endure during their lifetime together can only be borne through their united effort. So, too, happiness in marriage can only be created when both partners strive actively for it through a melding together of wills.

Here, each spouse is both bearer and receiver of gifts and only when both are united in harmony can they nourish that sacred happiness in which each feels they belong to the other.

Only when the wills of both partners are fully united can they stand strong together in the face of life's suffering and sorrows. And only then, too, can they nurture their highest happiness, so that joy flows forth from their union.

A marriage that has been strengthened by this shared intention will never be harmed by life's sorrows, nor ever be lacking in joy.

The partners in such a marriage will have mastered the art of limiting suffering to the minimum necessary in this life on earth.

They will know a joy that no sorrow can eclipse.

This steady joy, and the wisdom that comes from knowing how to minimize sorrow, will radiate from their marriage and shine on all those who come in contact with them.

Such a marriage will have a beneficial effect that reaches far beyond its own private sphere. It will create more good than other marriages in which both partners have long since forgotten how to make each other happy, and have not the slightest inkling of the happiness that could be theirs because, while they have been busy helping others, they have neglected their first and most important duty: the obligation to shape and nurture their own marriage so that harmony prevails.

THERE ARE THOSE who place great stock in helping others far away while they neglect the spouse at home. They heed the dictum "love thy neighbor" even as they drive their own happiness away. Contrast this with those marriages in which both partners value most the happiness of union—hardly realizing that when they lessen suffering and encourage joy in their own sphere, they are helping others as well.

Such marriages are sanctuaries of happiness and blessings will flow from them even unto future generations.

EVERY MARRIAGE should be a sanctuary of happiness in this world of suffering and sorrow. Every marriage holds within it the potential to reach such heights, so long as the intention of both partners remains dedicated to creating the pure, sublime happiness that flowers only from the union of two separate individuals.

Only within a true marriage can human beings attain inner perfection while they abide in this outer world. Only true marriage can work this miracle—marriage that perfects itself through the cultivation of happiness.

If humanity is to ever reach this noble goal, true marriages will have to multiply a thousand-fold, each fully conscious of its sublime power to limit the suffering and sorrows of this earth and to increase the purest joys.

CHAPTER FIVE

DANGER AND TEMPTATION

WHEN A MARRIAGE IS FOUNDED ON LOVE, the unity of the two partners is firm and deep-rooted, and only rarely can their shared world of feeling be shaken by interference from the outer world.

Yet no marriage is impervious to all temptation.

Temptation reveals the true nature of the marriage: whether it is grounded in genuine love or whether the partners have been drawn together for more superficial reasons, and can just as easily be drawn to a new and different person.

When a marriage is rooted in deep and true love, even the strongest temptation will not be able to harm it.

Even when temptation must be fought against and vanquished through hard struggle, love will triumph in the end. Temptation cannot win when the power of love is harnessed to defeat it.

Be on your guard, however, to spot temptation when it first appears, and do not wait until it grows so strong that it must be overcome through struggle.

You can train yourself to be alert to this danger—or you can allow yourself to become absorbed by it until it takes hold of you and now requires the mightiest resistance.

Temptation can cross your path anywhere, even though you do not seek it out and even when—out of fear that you may meet it—you carefully avoid walking on those paths where it might find you.

Temptation alone, however, is not a cause for guilt.

Only when you entertain temptation and let it come too close, when you encourage it and play with it—then, indeed, you are not free of guilt.

Even though you may emerge victorious in the end, you will have burdened yourself with heavy guilt, and should not rest until the consequences that flow from your actions have been made right.

You may well have to admit to yourself that you were not watchful where watchfulness was clearly called for.

It would be useless now to torment yourself for your failings.

No amount of self-reproach can undo what has been done. The only way to cleanse the stain is to make certain that your actions cause no further harm.

You should learn from every experience, and the fact that you have gone astray can teach you how to avoid guilt before the eyes of the Eternal in the future, even if you cannot always avoid temptation.

You must learn to notice and evaluate your subtle feelings, and if you detect that they contain the seeds of temptation, turn away from them at once.

If you can recognize the enemy the moment it comes near, then it always will be easy to overcome and you will never—literally—"fall" into temptation.

Only if you take pleasure in those first stirrings of temptation will you incur a karmic debt.

The struggle with temptation can make you stronger if you practice vigilance and learn to see through its many guises, so that you are able to prevent it from penetrating your inner world.

Every person has some sort of weakness, and temptation will always search it out.

But if you can resist temptation when it first approaches, and confront it with a firm and irrevocable "no," you will grow ever stronger just where you most need to be strengthened.

The practice of vigilance will change you so that temptation will no longer be a danger. Vigilance will become second nature; a habit so ingrained that temptation will search in vain for an unguarded entryway to slip through.

Only then will you feel secure and only then can you be trusted.

Only then will your marriage be sufficiently safeguarded, so that it may bestow upon you the inexhaustible abundance of gifts it has to offer to the man and woman who are worthy to experience its mystery.

❧

From the moment you commit yourself to create a single spiritual entity with your partner in marriage, you do not bear this sacred responsibility solely on your own behalf.

Marriage is not only a contract entered into on this human plane, although each partner has gained certain rights to the other, and owes the other loyalty even when they have been betrayed.

The vow a man and woman take to spend their lives in marriage is an event of cosmic significance. The marital partners are pledged to each other not only on a personal level but before all humanity, and their union reaches into the highest realms of the spiritual world.

Such a vow can only be dissolved when the couple is parted by death, or when both partners feel compelled to separate, for the most serious of reasons, and to revoke the vow they once made to each other, to all humanity and to the radiant world of the Spirit. Such dissolution may also occur when one partner abandons the other, or in some way makes it impossible for the marital vow to be upheld.

As long as your vow is still in effect, however, you are bound by the three-fold obligation from which no "god" can free you.

You will be held responsible even if, during this short span of time on earth—and indeed the longest life is short when measured by eternity—you believe yourself to be relieved of responsibility.

The fact that others give in to temptation and do not even try to resist does not free you of the karmic debt you have incurred.

You are responsible for your own actions within your marriage and no one can relieve you of this responsibility, even if others consider your deeds excusable.

Your actions may even be excusable in the judgment of Eternity, yet you must suffer the consequences of the chain of events your deeds have set in motion, and remain a prisoner of them until the last link has been broken.

Hᴇ ᴡʜᴏ ᴛʀᴜʟʏ had the right to impart spiritual wisdom once taught that those who look on another with lust in their heart, have already committed adultery.

Many people have found these words not to their liking, and have looked for ways to bend their meaning and interpret them more loosely.

I must tell you, however, that toying with or deliberately intensifying the subtle, erotic vibrations that naturally occur between men and women—when a person other than one's spouse is involved—is a defilement of the marriage. This is so even when erotic feelings have not reached the level of conscious physical desire and so do not constitute a breach of the marriage in the invisible realm.

Even if you allow yourself to be sexually stimulated by an image and surrender to it, you sully your marriage.

Yᴏᴜ ᴍᴜsᴛ ᴛʀᴀɪɴ yourself to behold beauty in the opposite sex with admiration and pleasure, but without allowing erotic feelings to arise.

Artists who find inspiration in the human form regard their models in this way. They contemplate the body posed before them, gazing deeply but without desire, and thus are able to experience a wondrous joy that stirs the soul—a joy that would elude them were they to gaze with sexual desire.

Artistic ability alone, however, will not protect the artist from enslavement to the animal nature; there are, indeed, some artists who degrade their art by using it to serve their lust. If human beings wish to master the animal within them and not be mastered by it, they must pursue the goal with purposeful intention.

IF YOU WOULD free yourself from bondage and learn to be the master of your sexual desires, then you must practice the strictest self-control.

You must evaluate sensations that begin to stir within you and, if you find them suspect, be ready to reject them firmly or redirect them into channels that are free of all eroticism.

Do not be mislead by the laxity with which such things are generally regarded. When people say it is "only human" to be overcome by such feelings, they do not realize that they are desecrating their humanity.

When you are unable to help others free themselves from bondage to the demands of their animal nature, you must be patient and tolerant until their time has come.

But if your effort to help others interferes with your first and most solemn duty—the sacred obligation to free yourself—then you must turn away from them and rededicate yourself to your own freedom.

I AM NOT TELLING you that temptation can always be avoided but, rather, showing you how you can defend against it when it nears.

Even if you escape the busy world, temptation will follow you to the most remote regions and will find you even in solitude.

You must train yourself so that you are prepared to encounter temptation at any time and in any place, confident of victory already in advance. You must become so certain and serene in your own will that, no matter how artfully temptation may entice you, you can no longer be aroused.

In this way you will protect the sanctity of your marriage and safeguard it from stain. You will spare yourself and your partner much unnecessary pain—even if it be a passing sadness that changes the next day.

THERE IS ANOTHER kind of threat to marriage, however, no less dangerous than temptation, that comes from the emotional realm. While temptation is triggered by something external, this threat arises from feelings buried deep within.

Caution is needed here as well and, here too, much harm can be averted if one recognizes the danger in a timely fashion.

ALL HUMAN BEINGS on this earth possess an inner realm that they hardly even know themselves, and which they therefore cannot fully reveal to others. It is not that there are secrets here that must be concealed, or something so sublime it cannot be expressed in words—rather, simply that human beings know too little of themselves.

It may happen that two people in a marriage, inspired by their deep closeness, feel compelled to reveal themselves completely to one another, and consequently open aspects of their inner world that immutable wisdom commands us to conceal. They may then suddenly find themselves disillusioned with their partner, and are aghast when they behold the twisted image of each other they themselves have fashioned by their mutual self-revelation.

They believed they must expose each detail of their inner world in order to be truly close—and then recoil in horror when they behold the naked "truth" of who their partner now appears to be. They do not realize they are gazing at a phantom—a distorted image they themselves have conjured up—and trusting it to be reality.

And so two individuals who felt themselves at one within their deepest selves now feel like strangers to each other. This because they wanted to speak truth in words where words can never speak the truth.

❧

A<small>ND NOW, ANY</small> chance encounter or event may suddenly give rise to doubts: Do we still "belong" to one another? The spouses begin to question the certainty of their feelings; they analyze and mentally dissect each other until, deluded, each imagines they have captured the true essence of the other.

But one cannot find the essence of a living being through dissection; one creates instead a phantom made of viscera—a shell that masquerades as the true self.

When the spouses show this product of delusion to each other, each one feels shocked and is repulsed.

Great harm has come from their great folly. Many a marriage that could have endured has been destroyed through this mistaken desire to be "truthful"—because the couple put more trust in words than in feelings, here where words lead only to error and truth can be found only in feelings.

❧

Nοτ οΝΙΥ ΙS ΙΤ unnecessary to try to dig into every detail and lay bare to each other inner regions that one hardly knows oneself—it is destructive to do so. Fixating on these obscure sensations gives them life; they take on vague and mollusk-like shapes that shimmer with light and then recede into murky darkness, shifting color and shape in the shadowy regions of our consciousness.

Words that are spoken in haste may have consequences that last beyond even a lifetime.

The vague and obscure impulses that live within each of us cannot be forced into words; words will only distort and exaggerate that which by its nature is inexpressible and unformed.

In the blind heat of fury, the tongue may spit out shrill and demon-driven words.

A moment later one may feel regret and wish those words could be retracted—even as more hurtful words are ready to pour from one's lips.

Words one never wanted to speak rise up from the depths with volcanic force. These words have the power to convince us, and anyone else who hears them, of their truth—although they bear no resemblance to the truth.

Once spoken, no power on earth can undo them, and no amount of apology can ever fully restore the trust that has been lost.

And yet, such words are nothing but the product of a wild delusion and those who speak them, thinking that they are getting at "the truth" at last—as if their past together was a lie—are deceiving one another.

All the more so because in the white hot anger of the moment, one's words are driven by the force of passion, and intentionally chosen to strike the hardest blow.

In retrospect, when looking at the matter calmly, the apparent truth in such impulsive words vanishes. One will often discover that real truth resides in the opposite of that which deluded thinking led one to believe.

Such realizations always come too late, and remorse can change but little now.

❧

ONE CAN NEVER fully repair the damage done by words spoken in anger and haste. Some memory will always remain, no matter how hard one tries to erase it.

How much better it would have been to have kept silent from the start and never given voice to things that by rights should not be spoken.

Those inner regions in which human beings remain forever strangers even to themselves are concealed for good reason, and one should never thrust them into the light of day.

That which requires peace should be left undisturbed lest it erupt in wild fury and destroy that which it might otherwise build up.

One must learn to master oneself even in the striving to discover one's own depths, so that one will not be tempted to plumb depths that are unfathomable and thus disturb the life that is gestating in the stillness, and must have unbroken quiet to take form.

In time it will become clear that every dark, confusing inner impulse is simply the transitional stage towards a completely different kind of feeling. Such feelings come into focus and define themselves through contrast with an opposite sensation and assume their

true and stable form by overcoming that
resistance.

❦

WHEN TWO PEOPLE are sure of each other's love
and yet feel compelled to constantly test one
another and ask for proof of their love in
words, they are courting danger.

They risk destroying the foundation of happiness they already have, and prevent it from
evolving and rising to still higher levels.

What your innermost feeling tells you is true,
needs no further proof in words.

Even when you feel confused by those dark,
vague stirrings that may rise and fall and
wash through you like ocean waves, causing
you to question feelings once securely felt—
you should not ask for reassurance.

Wait with calm serenity for an answer to surface from within you and practice silence
until then.

By maintaining silence you will master the
uncertainty and agitation you are feeling.

Silence will calm you and restore your inner peace, and you will once again feel secure and certain of your feelings.

You then will be appalled when you realize what words you might have uttered—words already waiting at the tip of your tongue.

You will be thankful that you remained silent.

Your silence protected your marriage from much harm.

Now that your inner calm has been restored, you may truly speak!

Happiness and blessings are yours once again and now the words you speak will bear witness to your renewed good feelings.

You will look back in horror to that dark day on which you were sorely tempted and in danger of cursing that which you now bless with your whole heart.

Because you had the wisdom to keep silent where speech would have brought a curse upon your marriage, your marriage will instead be truly blessed.

CHAPTER SIX

THE STRESSES OF EVERYDAY LIFE

COUNTLESS ARE THE "UNHAPPY MARRIAGES" which both spouses entered into with joyful anticipation, believing themselves to be entitled to every happiness, only to see their dream end in resignation and regret.

Alas, there are all too many reasons that can lead to such bitter disappointment.

The most likely cause of unhappiness in many marriages is the couple's unrealistic and naïve expectation that their marriage would be an endless, blissful honeymoon—that marriage in and of itself would bring fulfillment of their cherished dreams.

But marriage is most certainly not an endless honeymoon, and does not shield the married couple from the stresses and demands of daily life.

One cannot bask forever in the glow of love's intoxication, and forget the world outside one's private bliss.

Life has its natural rhythms; cycles of joy and sorrow that must flow through us like ocean waves, freely and unrestrained.

In the same way, the rhythms of life must flow through the marriage.

Even the most fortunate of marriages will only flourish if the couple is able to sustain their good feeling through the routines of daily life, and not just on special occasions.

Even when a couple is burdened by the needs of existence, they can still find happiness, so long as they adopt the right attitude. They should approach the daily challenges of life in the spirit of cooperation, accepting them as part of the rhythm of their relationship, and make space as well for times of respite and enjoyment.

To be sure, it is far easier to feel positive and pleasant when dressed up in festive clothes than in everyday attire.

And it is easier to relax and simply enjoy each other's company than to meet the daily challenges of life.

But marriage cannot always be carefree and exciting, a romantic "walk in the park."

Even when the partners might want to constantly express affection for each other, the struggle to meet life's basic needs and the obligations of daily life may intrude. And so, love must wait for special moments!

This understanding is, however, all too often lacking.

People often want every day of married life to be blissful and enchanted, and then feel cheated when it turns out to be ordinary and workaday.

And if this were not enough, it often happens that the spouses must spend much time apart, attending to different matters.

At day's end, one partner may feel energized while the other is exhausted, and needs time to restore a feeling of well-being.

At such times, both partners must try to discern each other's mood and rise above preoccupation with their own emotions. Much unhappiness will be avoided if the spouses can approach each other with an understanding heart.

Much discord arises when the partners are so absorbed in their own separate lives that they lose touch with one another.

If the spouses try to communicate by simply explaining their own situation, instead of trying first to understand the other's, both will end up feeling misunderstood and aggrieved.

All such misunderstandings follow from the stubbornness with which most people refuse to face the realities of life and the lengths to which they will go to avoid facing its demands.

THE CUSTOM of leaving for a "honeymoon" immediately after the wedding ceremony is problematic. It may turn out well, but all too often the newlyweds set out filled with joyful expectation and are disappointed when they return to normal life.

Removed from the demands of everyday life and free to luxuriate in each other's company, the couple begins their life together under conditions that will seldom—and more likely, never—recur.

It is all too easy to be misled into believing that such a carefree and undisturbed time together is indicative of how married life will always be.

The honeymoon creates a sweet illusion to which one surrenders gladly and which one wishes would never end.

But when the couple returns home, thinking that they now know something of married life, they are suddenly faced with mundane tasks and daily duties that may require them to spend much time apart.

Their own four walls may now feel as foreign to the couple as a hotel—except now they must manage it themselves. Life is no longer quite as easy as it seemed when others catered to their every whim.

For the first time in their young marriage the spouses are separated for many hours or even many days, and are responsible for tasks that had not previously been part of their relationship.

⚬

THE GLOW OF love's intoxication has been dimmed, and true love is now being tested.

It is not so easy to let go of the heightened joy and pleasure of a honeymoon, and face the mundane challenges of life.

In many cases, it would have been better if the couple had begun their marriage in the real world of everyday life and not in the illusory one of a honeymoon.

Nevertheless, one can say without doubt that something of real value has been achieved when the new couple becomes accustomed to their everyday life together—because only then can their marriage be considered successful.

⚬

PERHAPS THE two of you, who are now united by the sacred bond of marriage, were complete strangers not so very long ago.

You may each have been living your own individual lives with your own circle of family and friends.

And if you were living with your parents in your childhood home, you may have been surrounded by familiar family members devoted to your well-being.

Or, perhaps you both had already left your childhood home and found your friends out in the wider world.

Now, however, you have found each other and another kind of feeling unites you, different from the love of parents or siblings, and even from the deepest friendship. It belongs only to the two of you and can never be shared with others.

Do not think that this new kind of love comes only from the earthly joy of knowing that your bodies belong to each other.

If it is true love that unites you, then something quite different has come alive within you, uniting your bodies but also illuminating this physical union with a light that is not of this earth.

You are united now for your time here on earth, and this is your declared intention. Yet, two separate lives cannot be melded together from one day to the next, nor can the new entity that is a married couple be established overnight—although it be the noblest goal and highest hope of your young marriage.

You must be patient and tolerant of one another, and all your efforts should be directed towards discovering the differences and similarities between you and exploring how your lives have evolved to make it so.

THE PRESSURES of everyday life can be a good teacher here.

You will undoubtedly discover many more differences than you would like. And yet, if love will hone your perceptions, you will also see clearly those areas where your lives can most easily be harmonized.

You should with thoughtful intention overlook those things that have separated you in your life up until now, and actively seek out and share those that unite you.

Life will test you daily and present you with many challenges that can only be mastered if you both place your attention on points of agreement and ignore that which would pull you apart.

❧

LIVING TOGETHER in the same home will test you in new and difficult ways.

As long as you lived separately, you each had your own space, and could decorate it according to your own taste, and fill it with objects that have meaning to you.

Now you share the same home and even if your situation allows you to have your own separate space within it, to arrange just as you please, things will not be quite the same as before, when you were the sole ruler of your home.

You must now rely on each other in all things and love will surely move you to create your shared home in a way that will be pleasing to you both.

Many a treasured object will have to be given up and many an old habit changed for the sake of your beloved—if your home is to be a haven where both of you feel comfortable.

∞

No LESS IMPORTANT than the home you live in is the food you eat.

I am not speaking here of whether or not one should eat meat or avoid all animal products, or of other beliefs about healthful eating.

Those who believe it is a sin to hunt or slaughter an animal should certainly not do so—but they should also not delude themselves by thinking that this makes them better human beings, or bore others with "morally superior" beliefs that can be purchased for a dime a dozen at the carnival of human fads and passing trends.

In what follows I will not speak about what foods you should or should not eat but, rather, about the attitude you should take towards food, so as to harmonize each other's tastes and needs for sustenance.

∞

You EACH COME from different backgrounds, perhaps from places distant from each other, and grew up accustomed to the foods of your particular locality and family.

The foods of your childhood and the way they were prepared have special meaning to you, and this is how you would like to eat now.

In this aspect of life too, each day will give you many opportunities to adapt to one another.

The fact that I find such things worth mentioning may make you smile—but many a couple has learned from experience that even a meal prepared with great care and the best of intentions can bring discord to the dinner table.

You are a couple now, and have a duty to adapt your tastes to one another, even though you each have distinct preferences and dislikes for certain types of foods.

Often one spouse's favorite dish is distasteful to the other. Such aversion to a specific food is usually the result of an instinctive feeling that it runs counter to the needs of one's own body, and does not provide the nourishment it might to someone else.

It can be quite difficult to reconcile a couple's widely divergent tastes and food needs with the desire to dine together. Even the smell of a particular food can cause distress if it does not agree with one spouse's physical needs.

Therefore, each spouse must make the effort to discover the other's likes and dislikes—those based on habit and those driven by instinctual needs.

Here too, you will have to learn where your needs differ and where they coincide.

Do not imagine that such mutual understanding is superfluous or that I might be referring to those marriages that follow the curious custom in which only the husband's appetites determine what is served on the dinner table.

The need for daily nourishment affords the couple ample opportunities to bring each other joy and deepen the harmony between them, since bodily contentment leads also to contentment of the soul.

At certain times one may want to provide special treats, and not just ordinary fare—although I am hardly advocating over-indulging one's appetites.

It is little things like this that can bring much joy, especially when offered as a gesture of love. Serving a favorite dish, or fulfilling some special wish, has even more meaning when we know our partner has done it to make us happy.

Just as a wife will try to lovingly discover ways to make her husband happy, so too, a husband should find ways to please his wife with those small surprises women appreciate so much.

A little bit of extravagance, no matter how modest, will always make life sweeter, in marriage as in all relationships. One should enjoy it whenever possible, and not consider it wasteful or indulgent.

Now we are approaching a discussion of another level of hardship that may be encountered in a marriage—the stresses born of dire, bitter need.

I am referring to the arduous struggle to secure the basics of survival, those cases in which one has no choice but to work to exhaustion in order to earn enough just to meet the most urgent of life's needs.

Truly, in a marriage that must confront such adversity the love of the partners for each other is tested daily.

At the same time, there is an opportunity here as nowhere else for the couple to express their love anew each day, by offering each other help and thereby making the burdens of life easier to bear. Only love can lighten the load in this way.

Couples who are faced with the pressure of providing for the needs of existence must harmonize their lives far more than those whose circumstances are more comfortable.

If you would be a victor in this struggle, you must strengthen and maintain that harmony between you, here where it is most needed, and not allow the slightest impulse to weaken your resolve.

You can help each other at every step of the way. Even if you cannot help through concrete action, you can restore each other's spirit when it is spent, and give each other courage to go on, when it seems that all is lost.

Do not forget, however, that just as you can lift each other up, you can also be each other's downfall. If you think that adversity is made easier to bear by focusing on problems, or worrying if either of you has sufficient strength to overcome them, your negativity and lack of confidence will only pull each other down and keep you from finding the inner strength to rise above your troubles.

You can only truly help each other when you feel your partner's troubles as if they were your own. Only then can you carry the burdens life has forced upon you together, willingly joining with your partner and never adding to their weight by selfishly complaining of the toll they take on you.

Nothing could be more foolish than to bemoan a situation that you cannot change and to make it unbearable through constant complaining.

If, on the other hand, you are in a position to improve your situation, complaining will not make things better but will only sap your strength and dampen your resolve—just when you need your energies the most.

❧

No MATTER what pressures daily stress your marriage, they can bring you blessings if you meet them with the proper attitude.

And if your problems touch the lives of others, they too will be blessed or cursed, depending on the spirit that you bring to hardships you are facing.

Blessings and curses cannot flow simultaneously from the same source. You cannot bring blessings and happiness to the lives of those entrusted to your care if, through your own conduct, you curse your own life.

If you are able to master the stresses of everyday life and meet them with grace, the deepest desires of your heart will find fulfillment.

Then you will be able to celebrate life's joyful moments with full pleasure and draw from them refreshment and renewed strength, so that you may bear the challenges of life anew.

CHAPTER SEVEN

THE WILL TO
CREATE UNITY

HOW MUCH MORE HAPPINESS THERE COULD BE, in so many marriages, if only the spouses would make more of an effort to strive always towards a spirit of unity.

People greatly underestimate the valuable role that such a spirit of unity plays in ensuring happiness; otherwise, they would not disturb it so thoughtlessly for the sake of petty things. They would realize that insisting that one's own opinions are right and that one's own preferences should prevail is not worth the cost of damaging the priceless happiness in their relationship.

Any sort of trifle can endanger the harmony of one's marriage. If all the married couples who have seen the sacred vessel of their happiness shattered were to trace the path of ruin to its source, they would—far more often than one might imagine—discover that it began with petty grievances. Only later did they come up with other reasons, which they would not have even thought of had they not already become estranged.

I am not referring only to dogmatism or a stubborn attitude, both of which are simply ways of defending one's stupidity and a fossilized rigidity—and are anathema to all with open minds and free spirits. One can only pity those who hold such narrow views or regard them with a sense of irony.

I am speaking, rather, of those marriages in which the differences are in fact significant, but could nevertheless be reconciled if the couple were to face them with intelligence and try, in a trusting and loving way, to find common ground. Those who feel they would betray themselves were they to compromise and agree—for the sake of harmony—that black is white and white is black, are foolish indeed.

∽

You must be willing to let go of your position for the sake of harmony—even if you are undeniably in the right. In so doing, you create an atmosphere of goodwill that will make it possible for your partner to come to understand you at a later time.

Consider what your marital happiness means to you and weigh its value carefully against those things that would endanger it.

Then choose what is the closest to your heart!

Rarely will the differences between you be so important that you should need to sacrifice your marital happiness for them. Only if a compromise would result in grave and unacceptable consequences, would you be forced to risk your happiness.

In most cases marital harmony is disturbed by conflicts over differences that can in truth be settled in many different ways.

The best way to conduct yourself in such situations is by yielding to the other, because that is what is called for in the moment, and waiting patiently until your partner sees the error, or you yourself recognize that you were wrong.

In this way harmony has been preserved and your happiness protected, through the practice of a little self-control.

❧

Unity must be the firm and steadfast goal of your relationship, the lodestar guiding all your thoughts and actions. You must view it as the basis and prerequisite for your happiness together and neither of you may ignore this obligation to each other.

Much depends on your commitment to this goal.

In every situation that could lead to a disruption of the harmony between you, you must remember that the *human being* is the most important thing, and differences of opinion are secondary—perhaps even irrelevant—where human happiness is concerned.

You must never forget that points of view that matter greatly to you now may lose their significance completely at a future time.

Above all, understand that differences of opinion can never be resolved through arguing.

Even in those moments when you realize you are facing seemingly irreconcilable differences, and your hearts are pained, you will gain nothing by quarreling and trying to convince each other.

You will only deprive yourselves of the opportunity to build a bridge towards one another once again, where you may meet in renewed harmony.

Many a marriage would not have been destroyed if the spouses had put aside their differences and left them unresolved, trusting in the healing power of time, instead of being quick to do battle and defend the "rightness" of their position, matching injury for injury, exacting wound for wound, until the last spark of love has been extinguished and has turned to hate.

THE TWO OF YOU, however, who are just beginning married life, still have the power in your hands, that many longer marriages have lost, to spare yourselves much bitter disappointment.

Be wary then, of even your first quarrel—and guard against attacking one another.

As soon as you have quarreled even once—if you have allowed yourselves to descend into attacking one another—you have already lost much of your power.

To be sure, your love may have quickly found a way to heal the rift between you, but in the dark recesses of your mind, a memory will still remain, even if forgotten in your conscious thought.

And now with every provocation your unconscious prompts you to quarrel once again, and you succumb to its dark whisperings without quite knowing why.

Once a quarrel has taken place, it can become a habit. No matter how hard one tries to resist, the impulse to fight will rise up like a phantom that returns to life and finds new grievances to feed on—unless one buries it even as it tries to reawaken.

Therefore, strive with all your might to avoid even the first destructive quarrel.

It is more difficult to stop the habit of quarreling once it has begun, than to prevent it from intruding into your marriage in the first place.

Once quarreling has found a place within your marriage, it will resist attempts to dispossess it, until finally it seems impossible to live together without constant arguments.

❧

MANY PEOPLE do not realize that the little daily quarrels that have become a habit in their marriage can be stopped—if both partners are intent on doing so.

Just as the fox in the fable declares those grapes it cannot reach to be sour, such people try to convince themselves and other married couples that a harmonious marriage is a fantasy and means abandoning one's own desires and will.

Such attitudes are foolish. Those who hold that arguments must be an integral part of married life are ignorant of what it means to live in harmony with another person and fail to understand the sacredness of marriage.

So many times a small argument, that may have even taken place half in jest, became the impetus for far more serious disputes and led to the ruination of a once-happy marriage.

Wherever such a risk exists, one should summon all one's energies to maintain harmony in the marriage.

❧

NEVERTHELESS, IN the heat of the moment, one may at times be caught off guard and overcome with strong emotion—and even the best of intentions is no safeguard against this.

Like flood waters breaching a dam, an argument now erupts; suddenly flourishing fields turn to mud. You must immediately try to remedy the situation; it is never too soon to act if one would restore the peace.

Now more than ever, you must both be willing to come together in a spirit of good will and to help each other, so that harmony can return to your marriage.

You must never allow a situation to persist in which one partner continues to harbor resentment even while the other has made it clear that he or she is ready to be reconciled.

You should also not attempt to justify what you have done and so absolve yourself of all responsibility for what has occurred between you, out of a desire to protect your own cherished self-image.

Even more importantly, you should refrain from assigning blame and indulging in the fruitless search to determine which of you is more at fault.

If you now expend your energy in righteous explanations of why it is you lost your temper, you will only find yourselves embroiled in further quarrels.

The desire to "have the last word" and keep from losing face is always driven by the ego—although one may not be conscious of this motivation.

It often happens that one partner is ready to make peace and yet holds back, out of fear that this first conciliatory gesture will be rejected and one's ego will be bruised.

And so you face each other, unable to overcome your emotional resistance and unwilling to be the first to take conciliatory steps.

Now you who have just behaved like willful children would seek to educate each other. Outwardly, you hold to your position and pretend to be unyielding—though inwardly you have forgiven in your heart—because you want to let your partner know there is a price to pay for arguing, in hopes this will deter a future quarrel.

In truth, you should each feel a bit chagrined. Perhaps a bit of shame will bring you closer to each other and speed a reconciliation.

Attempting to make peace in this way will only lead to mutual torment and, unless some fortuitous external event comes to your aid and forces you to reconcile, you will sulk in silence and continue nursing your resentment—and miss the opportunity to find the way back to each other.

And now a gap that is already hard to bridge seems even wider and more complicated. You stand before it frozen and unable to do the obvious: to seal each other's lips, which have not found the words of peace, with a passionate kiss.

So THAT YOU may never have to wait like headstrong children wondering which of you will be the first to yield, I advise you to promise one another, at a time when all is well between you, that whichever one of you makes the first move towards reconciliation need never fear rejection.

You should solemnly agree that you will not allow your egos to become an obstacle to reconciliation. And whoever takes the risk of stepping forward first to bridge the gap between you must not fear that this move towards reconciliation will be used against them and taken as a sign of guilt.

You should also pledge that, once you have reconciled, you will not reopen your dispute and search further for its "cause." And pledge also that the one who has initiated your reunion shall not be viewed as the weaker person, who has simply "given in" and been browbeaten by the other.

Even if you cannot always preserve the harmony between you, the vows you have made will remind you of the need to move past the smallness of the ego, in service of the greater goal of restoring peace in your relationship.

It would be better, of course, if you taught each other by example, and with full awareness of your intent to do so, how to strive towards harmony.

Here too, you must lay aside your ego from the start.

It must never be an option for one of you to feel triumphant if, on seeing the other in a weakened state, you choose to step aside and not pursue an argument.

Rather, you should want to help each other in every moment of your lives and rejoice that you can do so. Do not allow yourself to feel superior when you have been the one to offer help.

The spouse who helped avoid a quarrel by wisely "backing down" and choosing not to add more fuel to the fire, may feel proud to have practiced moderation; but the spouse who was willing to be calmed and let the fires of anger cool is equally entitled to take pride in having regained self-control.

When you can both feel gratitude towards one another for the mutual good will that has allowed you to avert the danger to your happiness, then you have truly understood the value of your unity.

Here as well it is not helpful to have discussions afterwards about how the danger was averted, whose mistake caused the situation and who handled it more wisely.

Those partners who had lost control know full well that they behaved unfittingly, without it being spoken of.

The erring partner will be thankful if you leave to him or her alone the task of finding the most effective way of maintaining calm and avoiding confrontation in the future.

Nothing wreaks bitter vengeance upon a marriage more than the compulsion of the partners to humiliate each other.

Such mutual humiliation is the worst poison for a marriage, and can continue its corrosive work even after decades.

You should instead behold each other with respect and even when you see each other's weaknesses, never lose that deep respect.

Pay no mind to such weaknesses and do not speak of them, and do not let each other know that you have seen them.

Always seek to strengthen each other's confidence and, in the ways you interact, demonstrate respect for your partner and yourself.

Promise each other that you will pay attention to the good, the strong, and the positive in one another, and overlook each other's weaknesses and flaws.

In no other relationship are the consequences of confronting a fellow human being with their faults as fatal as in marriage.

⚬

THE LESSONS marriage has to offer each partner can only be learned through experience.

One should never try to "teach" one's spouse the way a teacher might instruct a pupil.

The wish to be seen as desirable by the opposite sex is rooted deeply in human nature. Every man and woman wants to be seen in the best possible light; therefore, the urge to "teach" one's partner or, worse yet, to clumsily point out and try to correct his or her errors, can only lead to ruinous consequences, even if these consequences are not apparent in the moment.

How can souls merge during physical union if the mind is disturbed? When the thought that our partner desires our body, yet is dissatisfied with our person, gnaws at the back of our mind, we cannot help but feel used and degraded.

No one is free of faults, but everyone wishes those faults to be overlooked when joining in sexual union.

Many acts of adultery have been committed by spouses who felt disrespected and seen always through critical eyes, so that it felt liberating to find another person, outside the marriage, who valued them—in spite of their faults—and saw them the way they would like to be seen.

Of course it is true that the challenges of married life bring to the fore different facets of a person and shortcomings that might never be otherwise revealed.

Still, all human beings want to be accepted by others—to be seen just the way they want to be seen.

In a marriage, however, the spouses will inevitably become all too familiar with each other's flaws. The best policy here is to promise each other to overlook such shortcomings.

Much suffering can be avoided in this way and much happiness brought into each other's lives.

❧

WHEN YOU HAVE fully understood all that is entailed in creating a harmonious life together whose essence is the shared joy of intimate union, then you will surely be able to keep your marriage free of strife.

As long as both your wills are joined in striving towards unity, you will be able to ward off any kind of danger.

Here as elsewhere, wishes alone count for little.

Few are those who would not *wish* to preserve the spirit of unity in their marriage.

And yet, in spite of this, there is so much strife in many marriages and, even in the best of marriages, much needless discord may interrupt the couple's harmony—this because the spouses lack the necessary resolve.

Often one is not even aware of such a lack of will, because the couple mistakenly assumes that "wishing" is the same as "willing."

Unlike a wish, the will to create unity does not rely on hope that what one wishes for will somehow come to pass.

The will to create unity is built upon the inner certainty that unity is possible and that it can be sustained.

The will to create unity is nourished by a faith that has no limit and knows it is invincible, even when danger threatens from all sides.

It is upon this will—and not upon your wish—that the harmony and oneness of your marriage will depend.

Thus, you must both resolve to awaken the will that sleeps within your wish, and bring it into active service of your deepest wish.

If you are united in the will to maintain harmony and oneness in your marriage, no differences or discord can ever undermine it.

Nothing will seem of equal value when compared to your happiness—and your happiness can only be secured if you protect the harmony between the two of you.

Only then will love find its fulfillment in your marriage—as it rightly should in every marriage.

Only then will your love truly become a force "stronger than death" and it shall endure even after this planet will have ceased to exist and its debris has vanished into cosmic dust.

CHAPTER EIGHT

HAPPINESS AS
AN INHERITANCE

WHENEVER HAPPINESS IS CREATED ON EARTH, it multiplies the possibilities for even greater happiness, as it touches all who come in contact with it, now and even into future generations.

Happiness can indeed be handed down, just like earthly wealth, to one's children and to their children in turn. In this way parents can bequeath their happiness—the happiness of a true marriage—to all who spring from their union.

From their earliest days children can feel whether their parents' marriage is blessed with happiness, or if it is clouded by conflict. They cannot help but sense whether their parents —the very people who gave them life—are unified or divided by discord and struggle.

Even though children may not be conscious of their feelings or able to interpret what they sense, they nonetheless absorb every vibration that emanates from those whose blood runs also through their veins.

❧

Most people are aware that good health and illness can be passed on through the blood, as well as abilities and talents and ineptitudes. But as yet no one suspects that blood is also the emitter and receiver of very subtle rays, undetectable to any instruments as yet invented, and which no instrument may ever measure.

People do not know that the quality of the vibrations transmitted by such rays is determined by the parents—by the time and place of conception and the course of the pregnancy —and that this connection between parents and child is inherent in nature and will continue as long as the parents are alive.

People do not know that there exists a constant, vibrational exchange through which the father, without consciousness of doing so, forms the child's soul—although the mother, from the first day of conception onwards, has an even stronger influence on shaping the child's soul.

This vibrational exchange continues even when the child has reached adulthood; the grown-up child may, through the choices it makes in its own life, block this interchange to a large degree or continue to receive it as before.

A kind of severing of this connection is possible here, but only if the child, by consciously and intensively refocusing its feelings, seeks connection with another person to whom it is drawn through the very same rays that emanate from the blood.

In such a case the exchange between parents and child does not completely cease, yet it no longer has a formative influence on the child's inner world.

However, this connection can be revived at any time through a refocusing of will.

THERE HAVE always been a few who have known of such things, although others suspected their truth; thus, people have long spoken of "blood ties" or of "friendships sealed in blood"—and there even exists the practice, among those who feel a special affinity for each other, of mixing drops of each other's blood.

If I am to impart all I wish you to know of these matters, I must speak more fully of those emanations of the blood. They influence the child from the first days of its life, encouraging it to seek that which is positive and will bring happiness or, if the quality of those emanations has caused the child's soul forces to be reversed, to be drawn instinctively to that which is destructive and will lead to harm.

From the moment a child is born, the parents are faced with the enormous responsibility for this new life—and they can only pass on happiness as an inheritance to their child if they have created it already for themselves.

Whereas earthly possessions can only be inherited after one's forebears have departed this earth, happiness and unhappiness can be inherited already in the mother's womb.

And this legacy continues to be increased or diminished until the parents reach the end of their lives on earth.

But the child's original inheritance, which was passed down to it in the first years of life, remains the most important influence.

Children may struggle with this inheritance later in life, either because they do not know how to value the happiness that has been handed down to them, or because they want to free themselves from a legacy of suffering. But whatever the parents have imparted can never be completely extinguished. This truth will be acknowledged thankfully by those who have the wisdom to build a life of happiness upon the positive foundation of their parents' beneficent influence, and will also be confirmed by those who must do battle daily with the shadows cast upon their lives by their parents' legacy of misfortune.

I MUST EMPHASIZE that I am still speaking here of the inheritance imparted to the child through the rays that emanate from the blood —and this influence is far more significant and has much greater impact than education and upbringing.

Whenever a couple has not yet found its own happiness, their child's soul is in great danger of being formed by radiations from the blood that are disharmonious and unstable. The child is then burdened with a heavy legacy that it is forced to carry throughout life and which cannot bring much blessing.

Parents who are poor in worldly riches often worry whether they will be able to provide for a child. Such children may absorb this worry already in the mother's womb and may feel unwanted even before they come into life.

Of far greater importance for the parents than financial worries, which can often be overcome, is concern about the legacy of happiness which they desire to pass down to their child.

Yet even this worry can be easily assuaged once parents understand their obligation to create a happy marriage, for then their happiness will naturally be transmitted to their child.

THE WAY TO create happiness in marriage has already been sufficiently set forth here.

I am well aware that this book cannot take into account all the particulars with which individual couples must grapple; still, I have covered all the general situations that couples face so that each may draw from my words the wisdom they need.

I am also aware that it is not possible for me, through these teachings, to instantly bring happiness to every married couple that has failed to find happiness thus far—for this great happiness cannot be achieved without the spouses' own determined efforts.

In no other relationship here on earth is outside help of as little avail as it is in marriage!

Only those who are willing to be taught to help *themselves* can truly find help in these pages.

This book is dedicated to such readers—to them and them alone.

THE CHILD born into a happy marriage will not only receive the inheritance of happiness that radiates from the blood of the parents, giving the new life direction and guidance;

this inheritance will continue to increase and grow within the harmonious atmosphere of the family home.

Just as words can only have an impact on a child's upbringing when they are backed up by example, so too will all the goodness radiating from the parents' blood be doubled in beneficent effect when the family home in which the child grows up and where it feels a sense of belonging is filled with happiness and peace. The child's soul is thus imbued with the sure sense that this positive way of living is natural, and no other way seems even possible.

When children born into such positive circumstances encounter misfortune later in life, they are able to rise above it, for the inheritance they have received from the parents supports them and holds them steady, even when the world around begins to sway.

Those who are nourished by memories of a happy childhood home, and who therefore know how abundant are the possibilities for happiness on this earth, will never curse this life, even if they are forced to endure bitter suffering, because of the actions of others, through their own actions or through no fault of their own.

They will find in themselves the strength to begin anew and will be able to rebuild their happiness, even from ruins.

THE TRUE WORTH of an inheritance of happiness is that it enables the heirs to create happiness for *themselves*.

It is an inheritance that can only be enjoyed if one allows it to permeate one's life.

Those who constantly search for happiness in new and different ways, will seek in vain.

Those who expect happiness to simply come to them one day, as if happiness is theirs by right, will also wait in vain.

No one has a "right" to happiness—and yet, all human beings have a duty to *create* their own happiness. Thus, we speak of people "making their own good luck" when fortune has smiled on them.

Happiness is never simply given to us—we must always create it.

Even the happiness that is handed down from parent to child must first have been created by the parent.

Likewise, the child may only be said to have taken ownership of such an inheritance when it ceases to take its good fortune for granted. Once grown into adulthood, the child must transcend mere delight and enjoyment in the happiness that has come its way without effort and recognize the obligation to actively build happiness upon this solid foundation.

Those who have grown up in a happy family home and so have witnessed how happiness is created, will best learn how to create it for themselves.

They will never lose this ability to create more happiness, building on the foundation of their youth—the legacy of parents who themselves knew how to nurture happiness.

IN THIS WAY, the happiness of a good marriage will flow outwards to bless even the children's children and will continually open new possibilities for happiness.

Blessed is such a marriage. It is a house of treasures whose wealth is never diminished, no matter how abundantly the joy it holds flows out into the world.

Everything else one may encounter on this earth is insignificant compared to the happiness that can be created within a marriage.

Most other things that we desire on earth are not solely within our own power to attain.

Such things are almost always subject to external forces and can be interfered with or destroyed by others.

How different is the happiness created in a marriage, for it is built upon the firm foundation of one's inner life and, once created, nothing in the outer world can shake or destroy it. And if those who once created that happiness wish it so—it will endure past death.

Just so, the legacy of happiness passed on to the child from the parent's good marriage will be anchored deeply in its inner life. No power on earth can ever rob the child of its inheritance, not here on earth or through Eternity.

CHAPTER NINE

THE BOND
THAT IS ETERNAL

ALL LONGING FOR HAPPINESS THAT REACHES up beyond lower earthly desires is a longing for the union of spirits that once existed in the Spirit's primal Ground of Being, which eternally creates them, and eternally releases them from itself in order to eternally return them to itself.

As yet, the human spirit is still imprisoned in its earthly, physical nature, which creates only separation where the spirit yearns for union.

Through the bonds of friendship human beings try to bridge their separation but, alas, friends will always remain separate individuals and never can two friends merge their inner beings and become as one.

Only in a marriage, where male and female join, can such an inner union truly be created.

Here two human beings are fused into a whole that transcends the separations of this earthly realm, just as they were once made whole by union with their opposite pole within the Spirit's realm, before the Fall into this world of physical manifestation.

Even though the individuals thus united are only rarely—in a few wondrous cases—conscious of the transcendent nature of their bond, this does not alter in the least the fact that such a union has indeed been established within the selfsame primal Ground of Being in which each was once united with an opposite pole.

Only the smallest aspects of Reality are revealed to human consciousness. Yet that which resides in the unconscious and remains unknown has far greater influence in determining the destiny of human beings than anything they can perceive.

※

THE VERY MOMENT a man and woman vow with firm intention that they will stay true to each other until the end of their sojourn here on earth, a new entity arises in the realm of Spirit.

This new and unified entity corresponds in all respects to the entity that existed when these two individuals, now unified on earth, were once united with their original polar opposite, within the Spirit's realm.

During this time on earth, this unified entity can only come into being through the joining of two mortal human beings. It does not matter whether these two individuals are in fact each other's original, eternal opposites, who were once united before their time on earth, and who will be reunited, in the fullness of time, for all Eternity. It is extremely rare for this to occur, and much more common for our partner here on earth to be a "stranger"—a polar opposite with whom we have not previously been united.

Partners in a marriage must therefore regard the one to whom they have given their pledge just as they would the polar opposite with whom they were united at their origin— because during this time on earth it is this partner alone with whom they are bound.

A new spiritual entity has been created by the spouses and not even the wisest can know with certainty whether the opposite pole with whom they are united during their time on earth is not also the eternal mate with whom they were united at their origin, and with whom they shall be united for all Eternity.

Only a very special spiritual ability can, at times, lift the veil that hides this secret, and then only with difficulty.

So as to leave no room for doubt, I must state here that even where there is absolute certainty that two human beings who were once united in the spiritual realm have now met here on earth, the new spiritual entity of which I speak can only come into being if these two individuals are united in a true marriage.

This spiritual entity is present always as a latent possibility within the realm of Spirit. It becomes awakened and is activated by the intention of two opposite poles here on earth to enter into lifelong union, and remains active for as long as that intention is maintained.

The moment such intention is broken—due to the death of a spouse, or the dissolution of the marriage—the entity it activated reverts to latency again, and will become awakened when a new and different intent to marry rouses it from dormancy again.

❧

ONE SHOULD NOT think that in the eternal realm there can be no "beginnings" and no "endings" and that, therefore, such cycles of becoming and dissolving are not possible.

One cannot penetrate the nature of Eternity by employing human reason; for the laws of this physical earth, which can be understood with our intellect, are not those of timeless Reality.

Everything here on earth, and everything in the entire visible cosmos, has a beginning and will also have an end, because that which assembles itself from individual particles must inexorably fall apart again. Human beings therefore assume it only logical to conclude that the eternal realm is simply the antithesis of this earthly one—that is, if such a timeless realm exists at all.

Those who make these "clever" calculations and presume that their "erudite" conclusions are based solidly on the unshakable laws of logic, do not suspect that they are measuring with a measure that does not exist in the eternal realm, and is in fact only the illusory result of certain thought processes, which give it the appearance of reality.

Eternity is solely the Being of the living Spirit; it is without beginning and without end and its essence is life continually in motion. The nature of Eternity remains forever incomprehensible to the mortal mind and the life of this physical world, along with all events in the physical cosmos, are only a distant, last reflection of the timeless world, dimmed by the crude, dark mirror of the material realm.

THE MARRIAGE of two human beings on earth is rooted in the Eternal, and draws its life solely from the realm of radiant Spirit.

Were it not for this connection to its spiritual source, one could no longer rightfully use the term "marriage." One would have to simply speak of the sexes joining, out of mutual attraction, in order to procreate and populate the earth.

If that were the case, cohabitation would not be subject to any formal rules, and individuals would order their lives as they wish. Social structures would be put in place only where necessary to protect the welfare of society, just as dams are built to regulate the flow of water and keep the land from flooding.

But so much more has been made available to us. When Male and Female fuse and become as one, human mortals are able to erect a temple that reaches upwards to touch the innermost of the Divine.

"Man and wife, wife and man, reach upwards to the Godhead's life." So wrote the librettist, a naïve knower whose wise and simple words, sung as if from the mouth of a child, were set to music by the greatest artistic genius of his time.*

Within the realm of radiant Spirit, the marriage of two human beings on earth is transformed into a spiritual event.

---

*The reference is to Wolfgang Amadeus Mozart's *The Magic Flute*. The words are sung by the character Papageno. The standard translation from the original German is "Man and wife, wife and man, attain divinity," however, this translation does not convey the childlike rhyme of the German.

Only in this way does a marriage become sublimely consecrated—not through words spoken by priests and even less through official recognition by government bodies whose sole function is the regulation of civil life.

We say that "marriages are made in heaven." In this simple saying, folk wisdom hints at the forgotten knowledge that marriages come into being in the timeless realm.

Even the power-conscious Church of Rome recognizes the centrality of the vow a man and woman make to belong to each other until death. It is this *vow* that seals the marriage; the priest's blessing only bears witness to that which the couple themselves have brought into being. The Church avoids making this position widely known even though it has been decreed by its own ecumenical council and, therefore, according to church dogma, has been transmitted through "the Holy Spirit."

The forms created as vessels for this ancient wisdom are still honored, even by those who have lost the key that could open the sacred tabernacle, for those alive today and for those who will come after.

Couples living in marriages that are formed according to this ancient wisdom should try to sense, in the quiet of their innermost feelings, that in a true marriage a mystery is being ful-filled—even if they cannot fully comprehend the glory that crowns each true marriage, whose radiance reaches up to heaven.

∾

EVERY MARRIED couple must gradually deepen their understanding of this reality, so that they may fully recognize that they are united in the realm of Eternity.

Here in the physical realm, the power of love is limited, because of the cosmic laws that govern life on earth.

That which is called "love" here on earth is only a faint reflection of the love that perme-ates the timeless, spiritual spheres—the love that is in God and is God's life, the love that brings to perfection everything earthly love strives for but can never reach.

Its clearest reflection in earthly life is experi-enced within a true marriage.

The greatest happiness marriage holds—the happiness marriage alone can offer—is this reflection of God's timeless love.

Wherever this clearest reflection of the love that is God's life is experienced by a couple within the physical-spiritual union that fuses two bodies and souls into one, there the realm of living Spirit has penetrated this physical world. One day, all human spirits will be united within divine love in the eternal spheres, but the man and woman who have come to know this unity in marriage experience it already here on earth.

WHEN SUCH A union of spirits has come into being, it will not be dissolved even when the polar opposites who were united before their Fall into the world of matter—but who have walked the earth in separate bodies, almost always unknown to one another—find each other once again in the eternal world of Spirit.

Within the spiritual realm, spirits interpenetrate each other. Spirits who have united with their polar opposites and have thus regained the state of being that was theirs at their origin dwell in mutual interpenetration with all other spirits who have also reunited with their polar opposites.

Spouses who have found the greatest fulfillment here on earth, even though they were not polar opposites who were united before their Fall into the physical realm, will most certainly not suffer unwanted separation in the world of Spirit.

Only those wanting to be separate will be separate in the spiritual realm, and even just the desire of one suffices to bring about such a separation, until such time as both partners attain the same high level in which all desire for separation ceases to exist.

At lower levels of spiritual existence, however, which must be traversed following the death of the physical body, the desire to remain apart or the desire to unite may prevail, just as is the case here on earth.

Where the desire to remain apart prevails, a mutual interpenetration will still take place, but neither party will be conscious of the other's presence. Whereas the desire to unite brings about *conscious* mutual interpenetration, a state of being so sublime that it cannot be described in words and is beyond earthly imagination.

If one were to imagine it possible to leave one's own body in order to feel every bodily sensation and stirring of one's lover's soul with greatest intensity and clarity—surpassing even what one's lover can feel—one would glimpse but a pale reflection of this sublime experience.

The deepest longing of all who truly know what love is on this earth thus finds fulfillment in the realm of Spirit.

∾

TRUE MARRIAGE can never be dissolved and continues to exist through all eternity.

It is not something that can be experienced only once in a lifetime.

When the death of one spouse ends the marriage here on earth, the surviving spouse can most assuredly enter into a new marriage and thus create a new union in the spiritual realm —without abrogating the first union in the slightest.

Jealousy does not exist in the world of Spirit, because the interpenetration of those eternally united in love, which occurs in the spiritual realm, cannot give rise to such a feeling. The jealousy of lovers here on earth stems ultimately from the soul's fear that the desired spiritual union might be threatened by another and will not come to pass.

In the world of Spirit, however, each spiritual union is forever sealed and nothing can endanger it.

All who were united by true love on earth will interpenetrate each other in the Spirit's realm and experience themselves as one.

Those once united in marriage here on earth may be physically separated by death, but will never be separated in the spiritual realm.

Within the realm of Spirit, the will to unity is strengthened and grows. It is this will that shall one day unite all humanity and it is this will that already unifies the man and woman joined in true marriage.

ॐ

A TRUE MARRIAGE creates an eternal union, not only between the two polar opposites joined in marriage but, also, in a different way, between them and all others already united for eternity within the realm of living Spirit.

Blessed are those who are able to comprehend what is presented here.

Blessed are those who are able to experience it in their marriage.

"Temples of marriage" should arise all over the earth—sacred places where the only priests are human beings who know of the possibility for spiritual union in marriage and are willing to strive for it with all their might.

Here, worthy advice on matters that serve the sacredness of marriage in this world should be available to all those who might benefit from it.

The external conditions that allow a marriage to flourish should also be encouraged from here.

Concern for the next generation should be the inspiration for all that such sacred places offer.

All those who love one another and who wish to unite in marriage should be able to receive kind and experienced guidance.

All those who have been unable to create happiness in their marriage and find themselves facing its dissolution should be offered help here.

Truly, great things remain to be accomplished, and all humanity would receive blessing upon blessing from the efforts of those true pastors of the soul—free of all desire to win souls for a particular faith—who are willing to help marriage on earth become an expression of its spiritual source in the eternal realm.

Humanity has not yet recognized that its real salvation is to be found in marriage.

People try to remedy one problem or another, with the best of intentions, but they do not seem to comprehend that help for all humanity can only be found in the spiritual energy that radiates from marriage in its highest form, infusing all it shines upon with the power of love.

No one seems to understand that the union of two human beings that brings forth new life is intended by nature and by the world of the Spirit to also be the birthplace of a new life for humanity— a spiritual renewal in which human beings learn the right way to live.

Where people are unconscious of the sacredness of marriage, where greed and lust run wild and are permitted to defile it through word and image and deed—often because those who guard their own marriages choose to look the other way—society suffers and is plagued by a variety of evils.

If humanity is not to drown in shallow, hedonistic pursuits and numb itself with excessive sexual stimulation, these attitudes must change.

Young people especially must protect themselves from this erosion of their inner lives, for they are the bearers of the future. They must awaken their souls to reverence for each other and for the sacred union that occurs within marriage.

A single generation that understands the sacredness of marriage and stands in awe before the most sublime of human mysteries can bring about the future that humanity has longed for and the noblest have envisioned.

Such a future can indeed be realized—but only if human beings will create it.

Only the will of human beings—and not their wish—can bring this miracle about.

Only then will many problems that seem unsolvable today find their solutions, and much suffering will vanish from the earth.

How very far we are today from this new age in which all human beings will be conscious of their holiness, the sacred dignity of being human.

And yet this new age will someday come to pass. When all human beings who possess the needed insight feel duty-bound to do everything in their power to speed its coming—that day will surely come.

Let no one think their efforts will be too small to make a difference.

Every single person's efforts contribute to and strengthen the accumulated force of will that is already present on this earth, and this will shall increase exponentially to reach the will of all.

Then all will say: Holy is the ardor of the sexes to unite in love!

Holy is the mystery of procreation and of giving birth!

Holy, three times holy is the union of Man and Woman joined together and living as one here on earth within the realm of time and then in timelessness for all Eternity.

REMINDER

"Yet here I must point out again that if one would derive the fullest benefit from studying the books I wrote to show the way into the Spirit, one has to read them in the original; even if this should require learning German.

"Translations can at best provide assistance in helping readers gradually perceive, even through the spirit of a different language, what I convey with the resources of my mother tongue."

From "Answers to Everyone" (1933), *Gleanings*. Bern: Kobersche Verlagsbuchhandlung, 1990

For a deeper understanding
of the core of Bô Yin Râ's teachings
you may want to read:

The Book on the Living God,
The Book on Life Beyond and
The Book on Human Nature

These three books should be
read together.

A description of all three books follows.

The Book on the Living God

The Book on the Living God describes the inner path that leads to birth of the Living God within--what we must do and what to avoid on the long journey towards awakening the consciousness of our timeless self.

Ordinary consciousness, Bô Yin Râ tells us, is actually like sleep; there is a greater consciousness that is alive in us, informing every cell, and our task is to unite it with our self-awareness.

We must also set aside the ideas we have been taught about an anthropomorphic God. God is not meant to be an external object of worship but, rather, an experience to be awakened within us. We are cautioned to avoid the pitfalls that might divert us: following false teachers or believing that certain foods or exercises, or ecstatic experiences, have spiritual merit. Everyday life, when lived with attention to the ultimate goal, will lead us towards a gradual awakening of our timeless self.

E.W.S. Publisher

Contents: Word of Guidance. "The Tabernacle of God is with Men." The White Lodge. Meta-Physical Experiences. The Inner Journey. The En-Sof. On Seeking God. On Leading an Active Life. On "Holy Men" and "Sinners." The Hidden Side of Nature. The Secret Temple. Karma. War and Peace. The Unity among Religions. The Will to Find Eternal Light. The Human Being's Higher Faculties of Knowing. On Death. On the Spirit's Radiant Substance. The Path toward Perfection. On Everlasting Life. The Spirit's Light Dwells in the East. Faith, Talismans, and Images of God. The Inner Force in Words. A Call from Himavat. Giving Thanks. Epilogue.

The Book on Life Beyond

The Book on Life Beyond is a guide to help readers understand what they can expect to find in the life beyond death, and how to best prepare for it.

Bô Yin Râ explains that life beyond is actually another dimension of the same life we know here on earth—just as real and solid, but perceived through spiritual, rather than our limited, physical senses. He emphasizes the direct connection between our actions here on earth and their effects on life beyond. We bring with us into life beyond the same state of inner being with which we departed, and are able to experience its wonders exactly to the degree to which we have developed our spiritual self. For example, those who have failed to show compassion for others and have lived selfishly will find that life beyond lacks the warmth and light that other, more developed souls can perceive.

Bô Yin Râ counsels us to mentally practice the "art of dying" as a meditative practice to prepare for the transition from physical to spiritual existence. The goal is to constantly orient one's thinking, emotions and desires toward transformation of the self, in order to be able to receive the spiritual help that will be available to us after death.

E.W.S. Publisher

Contents: Introduction. The Art of Dying. The Temple of Eternity and the World of Spirit. The Only Absolute Reality. What Should One Do?

The Book on Human Nature

The Book on Human Nature presents basic concepts about human nature with the goal of inspiring readers to awaken the timeless, spiritual spark within. We become fully human only when the spiritual potential within us gradually awakens and infuses our material, purely animal selves. It is a path that every human being may and should pursue.

A central understanding is that all life results from the joining of opposites, in particular, the polarity of male and female energies. Bô Yin Râ emphasizes that the true spiritual human being is male and female united in one entity; when we seek our spiritual self, we must call forth the male and female in ourselves and in all things. He discusses the biblical fall from grace as a descent from the spiritual plane, in which male and female were united, onto a material plane, in which male and female are split apart.

Bô Yin Râ warns men that holding onto the illusion of male superiority means forfeiting their spiritual life. While the spiritual paths that are natural for men and women are different in tone—open and receptive for women, active and grasping for men—they are equal and complementary. He tells us that *true* marriage is preparation for the life beyond: by coordinating the desires, wills and attitudes of two beings we once again bring about, in some measure, the original state in which male and female energies are united.

E.W.S. Publisher

Contents: Introduction. The Mystery Enshrouding Male and Female. The Path of the Female. The Path of the Male. Marriage. Children. The Human Being of the Age to Come. Epilogue. A Final Word.

CPSIA information can be obtained at www.ICGtesting.com
Printed in the USA
FSOW01n0814130516
20374FS

9 780915 034291

THE
KOBER
PRESS

The Book on Human Nature

The Book on Human Nature presents basic concepts about human nature with the goal of inspiring readers to awaken the timeless, spiritual spark within. We become fully human only when the spiritual potential within us gradually awakens and infuses our material, purely animal selves. It is a path that every human being may and should pursue.

A central understanding is that all life results from the joining of opposites, in particular, the polarity of male and female energies. Bô Yin Râ emphasizes that the true spiritual human being is male and female united in one entity; when we seek our spiritual self, we must call forth the male and female in ourselves and in all things. He discusses the biblical fall from grace as a descent from the spiritual plane, in which male and female were united, onto a material plane, in which male and female are split apart.

Bô Yin Râ warns men that holding onto the illusion of male superiority means forfeiting their spiritual life. While the spiritual paths that are natural for men and women are different in tone—open and receptive for women, active and grasping for men—they are equal and complementary. He tells us that *true* marriage is preparation for the life beyond: by coordinating the desires, wills and attitudes of two beings we once again bring about, in some measure, the original state in which male and female energies are united.

E.W.S. Publisher

Contents: Introduction. The Mystery Enshrouding Male and Female. The Path of the Female. The Path of the Male. Marriage. Children. The Human Being of the Age to Come. Epilogue. A Final Word.

THE KOBER PRESS

CPSIA information can be obtained
at www.ICGtesting.com
Printed in the USA
FSOW01n0814130516
20374FS